SURVIVAL
STRATEGIES FOR
NEW SCIENTISTS

SURVIVAL STRATEGIES FOR NEW SCIENTISTS

Carl J. Sindermann

PLENUM PRESS • NEW YORK AND LONDON

Library of Congress Cataloging in Publication Data

Sindermann, Carl J.
    Survival strategies for new scientists.

    Bibliography: p.
    Includes index.
    1. Scientists. 2. Science—Vocational guidance. I. Title.
Q147.S563   1987   306′.45   87-14193
ISBN 0-306-42703-6

PREFACE

The book *Winning the Games Scientists Play* was published by Plenum Press very late in 1982. Beginning almost immediately thereafter, and continuing sporadically to the present, readers have taken pen in hand to comment on aspects of that book and to suggest areas for further exploration. Numerous and extensive reviews in a variety of journals have provided further commentary—mostly supportive.

During this period of feedback, it occurred to me that the book had just brushed the surface of the material available and that beneath the skin were treasures of experiences in scientific game-playing that deserved far more than casual attention. The temptation to probe further was irresistible.

Themes for much of the material presented in this sequel were suggested by those who had read the first volume and who felt that much more could have been accomplished in particular areas. Ideas, concepts, and vignettes were borrowed freely from those commentators, and any other sources, provided they fitted the framework of the new book and the many prejudices of its author.

Reviewers of early drafts of some of the new chapters offered additional constructive comments (along with some gratuitous nastiness). Gradually, the whole thing began to take form as a genuine sequel to *Winning the Games Scientists Play*. Some of the familiar scientific arenas—professional meetings, the role of females, organizational bureaucracies—have been revisited, with keener insight and broader perspectives.

Writing this third and final volume of the trilogy that I call "self-improvement handbooks for scientists" has been a mind-expanding experience for me, which is a serious admission from a normally inflexible, buttoned-up New Englander. The second volume was *The Joy of Science* (Plenum Press, 1985); there was much joy in writing about good scientists and their folkways, and that has continued to be my experience in preparing this book.

I want to thank the Commonwealth of Massachusetts for providing superb accommodations for writing and reflection at South Pond in the Savoy Mountain State Forest high in the Berkshires. Without drawing too many analogies, I will say that South Pond is today's equivalent (at least physically) of the Walden Pond of an earlier time, located elsewhere in the Commonwealth.

Most important, I want to thank sincerely my Editor at Plenum, Linda Greenspan Regan, who found merit in the concept of a sequel to *Winning the Games...* and encouraged the expedition. Most authors are sensitive beings, trapped in a harsh environment, searching for small signs of approval of their products. Without the initial editorial nod from Linda, the pages that follow would not have existed. But they do exist, and I am content with them. Science—in and out of the classroom and laboratory—can be fun, and it can be exciting and rewarding if relevant rules are observed; this remains my central thesis.

Carl J. Sindermann

Savoy, Massachusetts

CONTENTS

PROLOGUE

A logical question upon opening this book might be: "Why do we need a further treatment of scientific games?" One reply might be that the playing field of games in science is so broad that a dozen books could be written and still leave some turf untrampled. A more reasonable reply is that so many fresh insights have been provided by readers of an earlier games book (*Winning the Games Scientists Play*, Plenum Press, 1982) that a sequel was almost demanded. Whatever the rationale, new and exciting material has been assembled under the title *Survival Strategies for New Scientists*. Some fragile guidelines were developed to aid in the construction of this new volume:

- More attention would be given to games that involve graduate students or postdocs, since the learning curves at these points in a career are particularly steep.
- The book would have to be a true sequel to the earlier one, in the sense that the material would

be an expansion and elaboration of some of the
concepts already presented, but . . .
* None of the earlier material would be recycled.

In addition to these general guidelines, a set of operating principles had to be elaborated, as criteria against
which each chapter could be judged. Here they are:

* *The games approach to science is a legitimate way to enhance the pleasures of a superb occupation, if the approach is built on a foundation of professional
  productivity and credibility.*
* Furthermore, *the games approach to science is not a
  cynical one and has none of the negative, abnormal, or
  pathological connotations that have been attributed to
  the term by many psychiatrists and psychologists.*
* Additionally, *scientific games are always very carefully
  ethical and never deliberately destructive or hurtful to
  colleagues.*
* Finally, *games are not merely idle pastimes for time-
  wasters; they are so much a part of the fabric of science
  that they deserve far greater attention than has been
  given to them heretofore by professionals.*

The thesis of this book is that "doing good science
is a worthwhile career objective, but there are *interpersonal strategies,* some quite complex, that enhance the
pleasures of doing it." These strategies I call "scientific
games"; together, they constitute a large and fascinating interpersonal universe that intersects the plane of
laboratory science at many points—a universe that is perceived easily and almost intuitively by some scientists,
but remains remarkably cloudy and obscure to others,
especially junior members of the club. Some call this uni-

verse "operational strategies" or even "manipulations." Others deny its very existence, insisting that science is too pure for this kind of approach and is concerned solely with acquisition of technical information; anything peripheral to that purpose is of no consequence, is a diversion, and is the domain of dilettantes.

It seems to this observer that reasonable skill in games is a logical component of "professionalism." Most of us in science like to think of ourselves as "professionals," but we rarely consider the meaning of such a designation—and in fact a precise definition of professionalism is difficult. I have wandered through countless scientific sessions, drunk from bottomless cups of coffee at breaks in those sessions, and accepted innumerable martinis at cocktail parties during meetings, looking for the prototypical professional. I know that he or she* is out there somewhere, and I can even describe him or her—as having most or all of these traits:

1. The professional has done and is doing substantial research and writing in his specialty—so he has established *credibility* and *visibility* among colleagues.
2. The professional transmits a certain "joy" about the science that he or she is pursuing.
3. The professional has high stress tolerance and high energy levels.
4. The professional knows himself to be good and insists on continuing personal excellence.

---

*Throughout this book, I will always be referring to both genders, but for the sake of fluidity in the text, I will use the masculine pronoun only (with the exception of certain instances when gender is denotative).

5. The professional is sensitive to human interactions.
6. The professional expects excellence from peers,
   and often gets it.

Scientists with this mix of characteristics are not abundant, but they do exist, and the novice game player has
much to learn by closely observing identified specimens.

Looking at the hierarchies of science, as they exist
in universities, government laboratories, industrial
laboratories, and foundations, the full spectrum of
professionalism can be seen as the pyramid is ascended.
The momentum of the upward movement is often
shaped in part by skill in interacting with colleagues, as
well as by increasing credibility as a producer of scientific information. In the end, though, professionalism is
a state of mind—an informed view of the universe from
the perspective of existing knowledge, however imperfect it may be.

Having said all this, I must admit to being, at times,
a little uneasy about the fragility of the statistical foundation on which some of the conclusions in this book are
based—in fact, I even have occasional small nightmares
about dealing with misconceptions rather than realities.
Are all these games just shadows on the wall of Plato's
cave, or are they real?

To reduce personal stress, several years ago I started
giving what I called "cocktail party miniquizzes" at society meetings, taking advantage of the small hotel-room
gatherings that are so abundant at most meetings. The
structure of the quizzes was simple: The questions (no
more than seven in any sequence) were crisp and to the
point, since the attention span of participants was un-

derstandably short during such events. The appropriate
point in the cocktail party had to be chosen carefully—
too early, and people didn't want to participate; too late,
and they could not be understood even if they did participate. The rationale for the timing of the quizzes was
that at such times, perceptions are especially keen, in-
hibitions are fewer, and hangups and biases are more apparent.

But, unfortunately, I had to give all that up. I took
so much abuse after about the second round of drinks
that I restructured the quizzes as questionnaires that
could be presented to groups, at various professional
levels, that were larger and soberer and responded
anonymously. I still get some abuse and resistance from
participants, but less than under the old system. A sample questionnaire is reproduced in Figure 1.

Questionnaires of this kind, as well as my constant
badgering of colleagues for information, insights, and
vignettes, have helped to produce an untidy mass of
data best characterized as "statistically insignificant and
nonrobust"—the kind of data that can be manipulated
with abandon, or ignored if necessary, to establish a
preconceived point. Such a happy combination of fact
and fiction forms the solid foundation of the chapters
that follow. Much of the content consists of interpretations and opinions, some clearly vulnerable to violent
disagreement, even ridicule. Accept or reject the ideas,
concepts, viewpoints, and flat statements as you wish,
but before you judge, think about the many interpersonal issues in which "doing good science" is permanently, inextricably enmeshed.

The structure of this book is based on a logical career progression from novice to journeyman to practi-

Instructions
- Check Yes or No for each question, indicating agreement or disagreement.
- Do not sign the form.
- Return the form to the moderator at the end of the session.

☐ Male   ☐ Female
_____
☐ Graduate student
☐ Postdoctoral fellow
☐ Faculty   ☐ Other (specify)

_____

Tier I. Frauds and the Pathology of Science	Yes	No
1. Have you, as a scientist, ever been tempted to "clean up" or otherwise modify data to fit a particular conclusion?	☐	☐
2. Do you believe that there is a large amount of cheating in science (e.g., fudging, ignoring, or slanting data)?	☐	☐
3. Do you know firsthand (not from published accounts) of any instances of outright fraud in science?	☐	☐
4. Have you ever been involved in a scientific controversy—either as a participant or as a front-row spectator?	☐	☐
5. If you knew that a colleague was about to publish, or had published, fraudulent data, would you expose him?	☐	☐

Tier II. The Female Scientist	Yes	No
1. Male scientists almost always appraise female scientists sexually on first contact.	☐	☐
2. Female scientists almost always appraise male scientists sexually on first contact.	☐	☐
3. Female scientists are considered to be equals (peers) by male scientists.	☐	☐
4. Do you know firsthand (by observation or involvement) of instances of sexual harassment in the science workplace?	☐	☐
5. The professional lives of female scientists still abound in put-downs and come-ons.	☐	☐
6. Flagrant violation of accepted sexual mores by		

FIGURE 1. Sample questionnaire designed to elicit opinions about professionalism is science.

a scientist can be considered as evidence that
the professional ethics of that scientist may be
questionable.   □   □

Tier III. Internal Journeys of Scientists   Yes   No
(To be completed by faculty members)
1. The assertion of having experienced "highs"
   has been appropriated by drug users, but of
   course has broader connotations. Have you experienced identifiable "scientific highs" during
   your professional career?   □   □
2. Do you feel that you as a scientist have contributed significantly to the development of a
   specific concept in science?   □   □
3. Have you made a major change in your scientific career (e.g., academia to industry, research
   to administration)?   □   □
4. Have you made major shifts in the direction of
   your personal research as a consequence of
   analysis of potential funding sources?   □   □
5. Would you include "joy" as a valid descriptor of
   part of the reward system of science?   □   □

Tier IV. The Power Structure of Science   Yes   No
(To be completed by graduate students)
1. One or more mentors have been of great importance to my development as a scientist.   □   □
2. Early success in science is frequently linked to
   a professional relationship with one or more
   successful mentors.   □   □
3. In the reward system of science, achieving the
   respect of colleagues and acquiring credibility
   as a productive professional usually outweigh
   financial considerations.   □   □
4. An informal organization exists within my scientific discipline, with an "in group" or "club" at
   its core. This core group controls much of the
   action within the discipline.   □   □

FIGURE 1. *(Continued)*

tioner. It is remarkably in accord with a perceptive statement made by Dr. Judith Ramaley, Vice President for Academic Affairs, State University of New York at Albany, at a recent society meeting. Her view was that a scientific career moves through three phases—(1) learning, (2) practice, and (3) mastery—and that as this progression is followed, people skills are important at each stage, but may become overriding in stage 3.

The book has two principal foci. The first concerns the needs, dilemmas, and emergence of graduate students and postdoctoral fellows—all in nine meaty chapters—with the premise that early acquisition of people skills must be pursued almost as vigorously as personal application to production of good science. The chapter headings give some clues to the major thrusts—from "Reaching for the Brass Ring" to "Recruitment." The second focus is on the people-oriented skills that developing professionals acquire as they move toward the peak period of scientific productivity. Here five more chapters—from "Characteristics of Science Workplaces" to "Changing Roles of Scientists"—lead down bright garden paths that are particularly relevant to this early part of a professional's lifespan. The other two volumes in this trilogy have considered the later phases of careers in science; this one is for the newcomers.

CHAPTER 1

REACHING FOR THE BRASS RING

Creativity and Productivity—in Proportions of 1 to 99; Standing at the Border—Expedition Logistics for Incipient Scientists; A Critical-Path Diagram for Professional Development

INTRODUCTION

One of the most pleasant and enlightening aspects of the background research for this book has been the opportunity for protracted conversations with many entry-level professionals: graduate students, postdoctoral fellows, junior faculty members, and even some recently hired industrial and government research people. The whole process of interviewing became a little more formal after some clever questionnaires were devised and administered. Further good techniques were extracted from a superb writers' conference held in St. Augustine, Florida, which emphasized the complexities of "oral history" (not least of which would seem to be proficiency in the use of a tape recorder).

After enough of these discussions and interviews, it was obvious that particular themes were being repeated, and some of them seemed important enought to be included in this introductory chapter. Understand clearly that this selection of themes is pretty subjective stuff—colored by the author's personal prejudices and misconceptions and hindered by possibly deliberate lies presented blandly by some interviewees.

Despite these admitted deficiencies, and other more serious ones that will emerge as the narrative continues, discussions with many junior scientists tended to cluster around these critical issues:

- The *overwhelming intervention of pure dumb luck in the selection of a career in science.* Probably the same could be said about many other occupations (except law, dentistry, or medicine, for which conscious career decisions might be made in nursery school—or by parents even earlier), but it is remarkable how often one finds a rapport with an inspiring teacher in an undergraduate course. Or perhaps one registers for a routine required course in science and discovers that its content offers access to the universe. Or one might sign on for a field project that offers unpaid volunteers (or even volunteers who must pay their own way) a vision of science as well as a lot of hard work. All these routes are traveled too often not to be statistically significant.
- The *rapid winnowing out of the best and the brightest from the average practitioners of science.* The first term of graduate school is an intense, highly stress-inducing, but surprisingly supportive proving

ground for beginning scientists. Very early on, it is apparent that some participants are obviously intellectually superior and are destined for great things; many others are merely excellent or very good and are slated to populate the solid core of science. A few others are not so good, and they will slip away early to other pursuits or will become increasingly frustrated by their lack of success in science.

- The *belated recognition of the need for a well-thought-out career development plan, once a choice for science has been made.* The formal steps in the hatching and early larval life of a professional are outlined later in this chapter. They are well defined and follow a rigid progression, but they should be accompanied by a no less clearly defined plan of *personal* development. Some elements of the plan are acquisition of experience in dealing with the people who form links in the ''system'' of science, improvements in day-to-day relationships with colleagues at all professional levels, and any needed behavioral modifications to enhance effectiveness in contacts with others. It is this secondary category—personal development—that shapes many of the real success stories in science and that is often slighted (even ignored) by incipient practitioners.

- The *intense pleasure in being accepted as an active participant in the ''adventure'' of science.* To some, this pleasure comes early, during late-evening discussions of science around a laboratory bench or in an off-campus bar; to others, it comes during seminar discussions or at society meetings; to still others, it comes after the first successful paper presentation at a professional conference. The important universal ingredient is a sense of belonging to a larger enterprise of the human mind and of being in the company of intelligent peers.

A few other themes emerged, but less frequently, during the discussions:

- The *overriding importance of a solid undergraduate foundation in science and mathematics.*
- The *importance of sensitivity to other people*—peers and faculty in particular.
- The *inevitability (and the acceptance) of hard work, long hours, and many frustrations* in the practice of science.

The most satisfying aspect of all my discussions with new scientists was that these were people who had recognized something worth the ultimate in dedication and effort and who had made a commitment. Some were more outspoken than others about the idealism, the expectation of excellence, and the required professionalism that are so much a part of science, but rarely did I have the feeling that scientific research was ''just another job'' to these young respondents.

CREATIVITY AND PRODUCTIVITY

Beyond the preliminary and maybe even simplistic generalizations just listed (the first of many lists in this book), it is apparent to me that success in science can be

shaped by numerous attributes of its practitioners. Dominant among them are *creativity* and *productivity*.
Creativity in science is embodied in the act of discovery. It is a concept more elusive than stress or entropy or ideation, and there are no simple answers to such questions as "What is it?" or "How do I get some?" Creativity or scientific discovery is often described as an exercise in problem solving, usually consisting of a series of steps, summarized effectively many years ago by a mathematician, Jacques S. Hadamard (1945). According to Hadamard, the major steps are:

1. *Preparation* (scientific background)—all the conceptual and factual baggage of a practicing professional.
2. *Assemblage and initial sorting* (often unconsciously) of countless combinations of facts and ideas relevant to a particular problem.
3. *Discernment* of that combination (or those few combinations) considered most likely to be correct solutions (this is Hadamard's critical stage of *illumination*, which is usually but not always a conscious process, requiring integration of available information, both theoretical and factual).
4. *Experimentation and observation* to verify or refute the idea, hypothesis, or concept.

Conditions that favor creativity include (but are certainly not limited to):

• Environment—which encompasses capable colleagues, a positive research atmosphere, and availability of facilities.

- A conviction that solutions to problems exist.
- Time for contemplation, free from too many diversions.

In attempts to cast the concept of creativity in simple terms that I could understand, colleagues have offered these descriptors—most of which disclose a broader, if still somewhat fuzzy, perspective:

- Creativity is acutally a *continuum* extending from recognizing a problem, to identifying possible solutions, to planning experiments to test the validity of the approaches, to conducting appropriate tests, to presenting conclusions to peers for their evaluation.
- Creativity is in part a mental process, but it often depends for verification on use of known approaches and existing equipment.
- Creativity must be defined broadly enough to include the often tedious acquisition and analysis of data sets from repetitive experiments or observations—adding minutely but perceptibly to a vast accumulation of earlier information.
- Creativity must also be defined with enough breadth to include attempts to integrate large bodies of data, thereby providing the syntheses that can be so critical to the evolution of concepts.
- Creativity is a unique combination of assimilated information and conscious efforts to solve problems beyond those to which the available information has already been applied.
- Creativity is a method of thinking about solutions to a problem; it is usually accompanied by tests of

the most likely solutions and a statistical examination of findings.

As remarked by J. W. T. Spinks (1975) over a decade ago: "We may have difficulty *explaining* creativity, but we can *recognize* it and *nurture* it when it is recognized." Spinks described creativity (unhelpfully) as "a gift of the gods"—which it may well be, but others look for something more tangible to explain its existence as an extremely variable characteristic of the minds of a certain subpopulation of scientists.

Still others (the more pragmatic among us) ask, "How much creativity is really needed in science?" and then go on to develop the ego-preserving thesis that a little creativity can go a long, long way, being quickly overwhelmed by requirements for verification by extensive data-gathering—concluding that this more mundane activity is the real essence of scientific research.

Following this escapist line of reasoning, we can skirt the too nebulous subject of creativity at this point and move quickly to the second major contributor to success in science—*productivity*. This is a subject that must be confronted directly, since it is the bedrock of a professional career. Some scientists may perform brilliantly on the public stage or function smoothly as managers or administrators, but all must face the inflexible measure of *production of new information* as an ultimate criterion of worth and credibility as a scientist.

"But," you will certainly say, "what of those scientists who are excellent teachers and who prefer to invest their time in course improvement?" "What of those who develop good rapport with many graduate students and

spend much of their time in discussions of thesis research?" "What of those who develop reputations as ac-
tivists in current science-related issues, often at the
expense of an aggressive personal research program?"
"What of those who spend inordinate amounts of time
writing research proposals for funding to support asso-
ciates, postdocs, relatives, technicians, and high school
dropouts?" "What of those with good synthetic abilities,
who write reviews and textbooks but do little original research?" The hard answer, from my obviously biased
perspective, is always the same: "*The essence of being a
scientist is to produce and publish new technical information.*"
Other science-associated accomplishments may be com-
mendable, and even noteworthy, but only as *adjuncts*;
they do not supplant the primary criterion of research
productivity. To some, this measure of worth as a scientist may seem too harsh and too narrow, but in innumerable discussions with colleagues about the real arbiter of
success—the judgment of peers—productivity always
stands tall.

As a grudging concession to fairness, however, I admit that other points of view have been expressed—
especially those that sketch the "scientist" with a much
broader perspective. Current science is a complex enterprise, requiring cadres of professionals with science back-
grounds to plan and administer government programs,
to review grant proposals and award funds, to translate
technical findings into everyday language—to perform all
the *supporting* functions that allow research scientists to
get on with the essential production of new information.
Many professionals in these supporting roles consider
themselves to be practicing scientists and deeply resent
any implication that they are any less important to the

total scientific endeavor than their colleagues at the benches or in the classrooms. Some of my best friends are what can be called "hyphenated scientists"— scientist-administrators, scientist-managers, scientist-politicians, or scientist-entrepreneurs—so any extreme positions in defining a scientist or evaluating his or her worth can be risky.

All this is an oblique and even mildly confusing way of approaching a basic problem for most scientists (and especially for newer ones)—how to be creative and productive, how to contribute to concept development and to maintain research output—when faced with the many frustrations and diversions that are encountered every day. I wish a clear solution to the problem existed, but all I can offer are some observations in the following section.

EXPEDITION LOGISTICS

It is easy to find good reasons for electing a career in science. Some of them may seem just a tad too idealistic or starry-eyed even though they may be valid. There is, for example, a certain exhilaration to be gained from performing at the boundaries of human understanding— at the borders of the unknown or previously misunderstood. In an era and a world in which idealism seems in short supply and is often equated with naïveté, just knowing that a job can be exhilarating is cause for some minor celebration.

For all its pleasurable aspects, however, scientific research requires perseverance in the face of constant frustrations. It is hard, demanding work; often, each tiny

insight is torn painfully from the unknown; almost as often, findings prove to be wrong or inconclusive or con-
tradictory, despite all the struggle to get them. Once in
a while, though, an experiment works or an observation
fits a pattern. It is at these moments that the correctness
of a science career choice is reaffirmed and the risks of
border-crossings are justified.

Once a decision for science as a career has been
made, an action plan is necessary, preferably in writing,
including an optimistic timetable, alternative paths, and
redundant circuits—the last as insurance against the
guaranteed intervention of random events that can
modify, disrupt, or destroy the plan.

Integral to the plan is an objective assessment of basic personal equipment that is on hand or has to be acquired. Since this is an age of quizzes and questionnaires, I have devised a highly simplified series of
questions with an even simpler scoring system that
will give the illusion of reducing the subjectivity of what
is clearly a very personal decision. Some sections of the
questionnaire are duplicated in Figure 2. Scoring the
results, allowing 2 points for each "Good," answer, 1
for each "So-so," and 0 for each "Terrible," and using
a pass/fail system, a score of 15 or higher puts you with
the near-geniuses (or the wearers of rose-colored
glasses), 10 is a minimum passing grade, and a score
lower than 10 is a strong clue that your future is in some
occupation other than science.

With the assumptions that a passing grade has been
made on the questionnaire and that none of the foregoing admonitions or encouragements has had any impact
on personal decision-making by the potential scientist,
a final attempt at order and rational thinking takes the
form of a so-called "critical-path" diagram (Figure 3) es-

| | My opinion | | |
Criterion	Good	So-so	Terrible
1. Genuine, even overriding, interest in the subject matter of science	☐	☐	☐
2. Reasonable to good undergraduate record, preferably including senior honors thesis or equivalent	☐	☐	☐
3. Interest in discovery through inquiry	☐	☐	☐
4. Suspicion of the superficial and the dogmatic	☐	☐	☐
5. Some reasonable hope for substantial financial subsidy (e.g., parents, job)	☐	☐	☐
6. Willingness to persist in long-term projects, and an extraordinarily high tolerance for frustration	☐	☐	☐
7. At least marginal quantitative capabilities and a good foundation in mathematics	☐	☐	☐
8. Early contact with the machines scientists use—especially some familiarity with computers and their potential applications to research	☐	☐	☐
9. Extraordinary flexibility	☐	☐	☐
10. An established reputation for self-motivation and freedom from the sixth deadly sin (sloth)	☐	☐	☐

FIGURE 2. Self-evaluation questionnaire for prospective scientists.

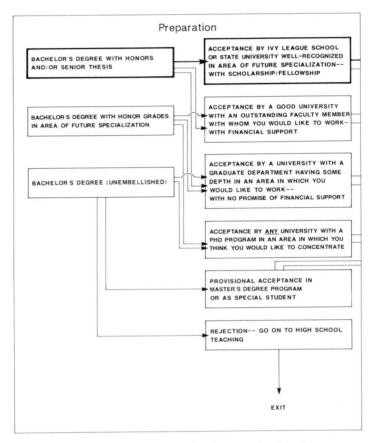

F<small>IGURE</small> 3. Critical-path diagram for developing scientists (in seven easy stages).

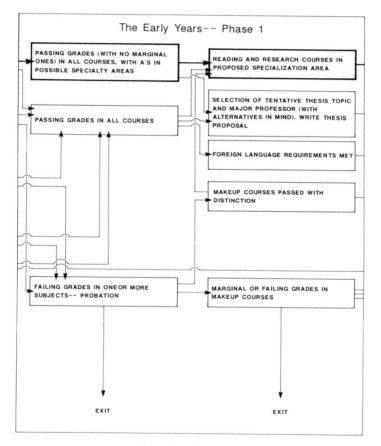

FIGURE 3. *(Continued)*

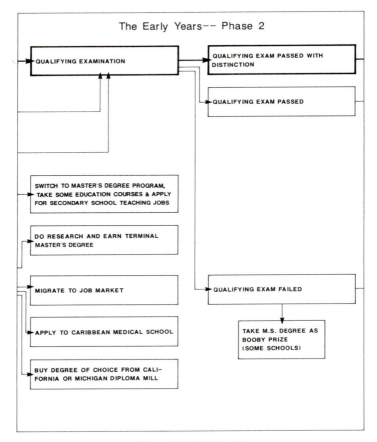

FIGURE 3. (Continued)

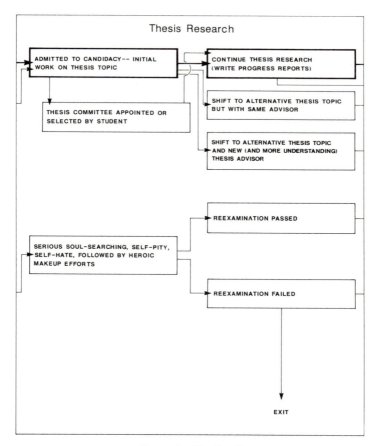

FIGURE 3. *(Continued)*

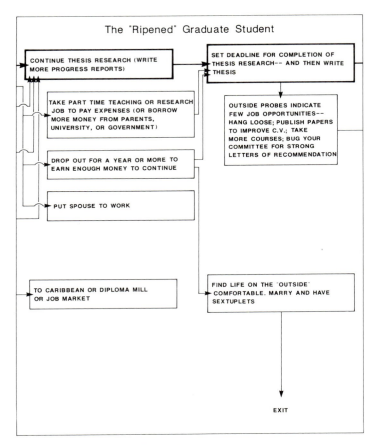

FIGURE 3. *(Continued)*

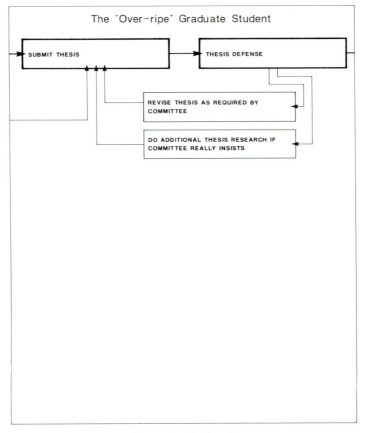

FIGURE 3. *(Continued)*

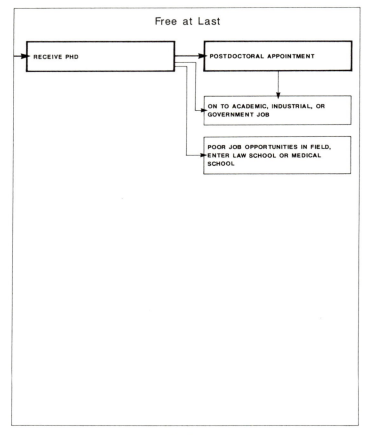

FIGURE 3. (Continued)

pecially designed for those individuals with nonverbal tendencies. The diagram is "multipurpose," in that it depicts a straight-line route for the obvious winners, but also explores the alternate journeys and the departure points for the less favored. The illustration is a composite that fits most graduate schools; the paths may be modified slightly by special requirements of some institutions, but only in detail, not in substance.

Figure 3 is presented in seven panels, representing seven phases of graduate student existence. The panels have been designed so that they can be copied (my apologies to the publisher) and carefully placed side by side to form the entire continuum of graduate education. Once assembled, the panels can be mounted on cork board for use with colored pins to mark progress or as a dart board by those who have difficulty reaching decisions by any other method.

Here, then, all too briefly, are a few of the ingredients required for a career in science—some idealism mixed with at least an attempt at appraisal of fitness, a soupçon of creativity combined with a large portion of productivity, and a development plan with some flexibility. There are, however, no guarantees of success. Even when the logistics seem in order, there is still the major ingredient of adeptness in personal relationships—which is what the rest of this book is all about.

CHAPTER 2

COMPORTMENT, DEPORTMENT, AND OTHER DANCES WITHIN THE IVORY TOWER

Probing the Realities of Student–Faculty Boundaries; Coping with the Harassed Department Chairman; Negotiating with the University Administration; The Teaching Fellow in Sickness and Health; Ethics for Beginners; Intuition for Graduate Students; A Sampler of Graduate Student Dilemmas; Behavioral Aspects of Social Functions

INTRODUCTION

The background research for this chapter on comportment and deportment included computer and other searches for handbooks, guidelines, instructional pamphlets, xeroxed handouts, and other literature explaining generally accepted "good manners" in research and/or teaching institutions—especially for aids useful to beginning scientists. Predictably, no such body of literature could be found (at least not with the retrieval methods used); the subject matter is clearly not "technical" in the usual sense, nor is it a research area that might prove particularly enticing to the average sociologist or psychologist. We are thus left needing a great fund of necessary behavioral information for the new scientist to acquire by observation of role models, by instruction at the knee of the major professor, by trial and error, or *never to be acquired at all.* This is an appalling condition, not to be tolerated by good, upwardly mobile scientists, since some of that upward mobility may well depend on appropriate responses to personal encounters within the institution (university department, research laboratory, foundation, field station, or other assemblages of professionals).

A logical but naïve question that should be asked by every incipient scientist is: "Where are my instruction sheets for guidance in critical interpersonal areas, such as coping with department chairmen, loyalty versus freedom of choice in research/teaching organizations, ethical behavior of scientists, scientific group social activities, and a long list of similar topics?" Fortunately, for those who may feel deprived by the absence of such self-improvement literature, this chapter attempts one small but no doubt welcome remedial step to correct a universal deficiency. A chapter is not enough; an entire book on the topic is called for, but this is a beginning. Of the many philosophical and practical issues that could be confronted, a mere half dozen or so, considered most relevant to new scientists, have been chosen for some preliminary discussion, clustered under the following general topic areas:

- Realities of student–faculty boundaries
- Coping with department chairmen

- Dealing with the administration
- Teaching fellowships
- Ethics
- Graduate student dilemmas

This list is clearly only the top scoop of ice cream in the cone; much empty air space beneath it needs to be filled.

PROBING THE REALITIES OF
STUDENT–FACULTY BOUNDARIES

The scientific community seems to function with some modest inefficiency most of the time, but it does best when its members live by general rules of conduct. These rules will not be found posted on any bulletin board or inscribed on any museum wall, and there is remarkably little unanimity of support for them among professionals, but they help fend off total chaos in research and teaching institutions. They are unwritten and, being so, can be ignored, modified, accepted, accepted with reservations, rejected, rejected violently, interpreted, misinterpreted, used for selfish advantage, ridiculed, abused, hailed, or hated. Some concern the *practice* of science—acceptable tests for statistical validity of data, critical evaluation of the findings of others, acceptance of ethical procedures in experimentation, and many others—while some concern the innumerable *personal interactions* associated with the practice of science.

The boundaries that separate graduate students from faculty constitute an important area in which unwritten rules apply. Superficially, the borders seem clearly defined: relatively permanent paid appointed faculty on one side, transient paying students on the other. The distinctions can get fuzzy, though, and this blurring can create problems for unwary or overly aggressive students. Consider these examples:

Bob Warner is a bright, congenial Assistant Professor of Physiology, only three years beyond his Ph.D. Because of his youthful appearance and friendliness, some graduate students respond with overfamiliarity, such as calling him by his first name or dropping into his office for informal chats at any time. He secretly resents these minor transgressions, but has chosen to ignore them in order to retain the kind of intimate contact that is important to his style of teaching. He will admit, though, to slight twinges of stress when these overfamiliarities occur.

The take-home lesson here for graduate students has to be to accept the reality of a boundary, regardless of implied invitations to scale the wall, because even if the faculty member involved does not object, some of his or her colleagues—those who like the concept of a wall, or at least a defined boundary—may feel threatened.

Joan Royston is a newly appointed Assistant Professor in the physics department of a relatively small private university. She has been developing graduate and undergraduate courses in her specialty area and applying vigorously for grants to support her research. Her professional manner is correct, but somewhat reserved and impersonal insofar as student contacts are concerned. Some graduate students resent this, as evidence of insensitivity to their needs, and have commented to other faculty members and the Department Chairman about it. The comments have reached her indirectly, increasing the level of insecurity normal for a new staff member, but not resulting in improvement in her rapport with the students. She is remarkably well qualified in her field and is now considering a full-time research position at a nonteaching institution.

Some graduate students are uneasy about their role in what may be construed as meddling in faculty affairs and possibly depriving the university of talents. Others feel that this is a legitimate use of student power, if their best interests are to be served—regardless of the boundary concept.

Mitchell Small is one of a small proportion of Ph.D.'s who remain at their degree-granting institutions as faculty members. Before receiving his degree, he applied for a prestigious two-year postdoctoral fellowship that was approved. The grant-supported research was exceptional, and on its termination he was offered, and he accepted, an Assistant Professor position. He is a normally congenial and assertive person, who had excellent peer relationships as a graduate student, but he is somewhat disturbed about his status as a former student and present faculty member. He finds, with some justification, that he is still considered a ''student'' by some senior faculty members, even though he crossed the boundary two years ago. His acceptance as a faculty colleague and academic partner has been, in his estimation, slow and reluctant—to the point where he has concluded that he must move to another university if he is ever to achieve a measure of professional recognition by department members.

These examples of ''boundary'' problems illustrate the pervasiveness of the need to sort out interpersonal relationships in academic settings. In the case of Dr. Warner, it seems clear that some behavioral modifications are in order—that for his own peace of mind, he can't continue to be ''one of the boys.'' He needs to accept the role change and act accordingly, despite his

natural inclinations. Dr. Royston has the reverse
problem—how to appear more like a concerned human
being in her contacts with students. This may take some
effort because of her normally somewhat impersonal
manner, but should be tractable. Dr. Small's problem is
a more difficult one, and moving to a new environment
may be the best solution. The passage of time may
modify colleagues' attitudes, but probably too slowly
from his perspective.

There is no correct or ideal solution to any of the problems presented in the examples, and of course the cir-
cumstances vary from one situation to another. The only
common ingredient is the demonstration that an ephemeral boundary *does* exist between student and faculty
member, so awareness of its reality and its general location can help determine proper etiquette.

COPING WITH DEPARTMENT CHAIRMEN

Perceptive graduate students persist in attempts to
empathize with, or at least to communicate with, their
Department Chairmen. Such jobs are held by highly
harassed individuals, expected to keep order among un-
ruly and often unreasonable faculty members and to
maintain a personal research and teaching schedule as
well—at least in smaller departments. They are responsible for actions of professionals over whom they have
remarkably little direct control. Their responsibilities ex-
tend to creating departmental cohesiveness and "esprit,"
encouraging a high degree of scholarly productivity and
grant-supported research by faculty members, settling in-
tradepartmental squabbles and faculty complaints with
tact, and interacting with the administrative hierarchy of

the university, especially the Dean, who is an immediate supervisor in the official definition of the term.

Care and feeding of graduate students is an additional responsibility of the job, but fortunately one that can be handed off to the graduate faculty, except for crisis situations. The Chairman thus becomes one step removed from the flow of graduate student activity—always available theoretically, but in practice relating through a faculty member. This is a reality to be kept clearly in mind by graduate students wanting some access to the Chairman. The route in both directions is customarily through a major professor/thesis advisor. Of course, the rigidity or flexibility of this "chain of command" system is at the option of the Chairman, and individual preferences vary widely. In some departments, he or she is easily accessible to faculty and students alike, and personally concerned; in others, the Chairman can seem remote and unconcerned, especially in instances in which student problems are involved. Reeducation of Chairmen in the latter category is feasible if handled with great sensitivity and if pursued through faculty intermediaries—never by one-on-one or group confrontation tactics. Most Department Chairmen that I have known have been appointed to their jobs, or had the jobs thrust upon them, with little training or even clear definition of duties. Each incumbent adopts a comfortable operational style regardless of its shortcomings. These are all intelligent people, and they expect to grow into the new responsibilities. The open-minded Chairman welcomes advice and comment, properly couched and delivered through appropriate channels. The more ego-deficient of them try to establish petty dictatorships (the Papa-Doc Syndrome) during their tenures and may have scant interest in suggestions from students.

NEGOTIATING WITH "THE ADMINISTRATION"

A classic love–hate relationship exists between the university administration and the graduate student population. On one hand, the administration hierarchy (ascending upward from the Department Chairman) must ensure effective education, adequate communication, and minimal chaos, while still suppressing overt or subversive student attempts to take control. On the other hand, the students must keep the administration from expressing its natural dictatorial tendencies without undue disruption of the academic process (and without resorting to actions leading to dismissal).

The dynamic nature of the relationship usually leads to formation of graduate student organizations with members designated to take the lead and the heat in discussions or negotiations with the administration and the faculty. The roles of representatives may include membership on student–faculty academic oversight committees, student membership on university faculty senates or similar bodies, and (in extremis) participation in bargaining sessions to reduce hostilities and impacts of protest meetings or student strikes.

The extent of student activism at the graduate level is always subject to debate; perspectives vary remarkably depending on which side of the academic fence the respondent is found—and even within the herd on either side. Ideally, any action is designed to improve the students' status and bargaining position and ultimately the level of graduate education—but sometimes things get out of hand and the matter degenerates into a confrontation rather than a cooperative venture. The losers at this level are almost always the activist students and their supporters. Administrators may not be smarter, but they are usually more experienced, and *they are in charge*. The bottom line has to be the simplistic one, that the students and administrators must be *partners* and not *antagonists* in affairs that affect graduate education—and that communication has to be continuous if the whole relationship is to be a successful one.

The delicious feeling of power—new to many graduate students—derived from participating in decisions that affect the nature and quality of their education is a heady one. Unfamiliarity with the abuses of power may lead to occasional excesses that can be destructive.

JOYS AND SORROWS OF
TEACHING FELLOWSHIPS

To be an absolutely superb teaching fellow, rather than just another run-of-the-laboratory "T.A.," is one of the most important career decisions that any graduate student can make. Experience on the job can provide insights about depth of interest and potential abilities in college teaching that can be gained in no other way. A fair test, however, requires serious time-consuming physical and mental preparation for lab sessions, attendance at *all* the course lectures, and conferences with students—not an easy regime, since it is superimposed on all the other demands on the time of graduate students.

At Harvard, at a time before the almost total integration of Radcliffe students (and that will really date me), the Crimson *published an annual critique and assessment of faculty and teaching fellows for the enlightenment of new undergraduates. A nostalgic review of comments about teaching fellows made in those simpler and purer days (with separate and proper lab sections for females) discloses a list of comments and gripes, which I can recall dimly, about the quality of teaching that are still relevant to lab instruction today (we learn so slowly):*

- *"Some teaching fellows seem to know less about the subject matter than I do" (these are Bio 1 students, remember).*
- *"Some teaching fellows have bad breath and need a shave and a clean shirt" (at Harvard, yet).*
- *"Some teaching fellows are remarkably smug about their tiny hoard of technical information and dole it out with great disdain."*
- *"Some teaching fellows will go to remarkable distances of obfuscation to avoid admitting that they just don't know."*

But the flipside has to be mentioned. Those same yellowing Crimson *pages also contain comments from undergraduates about exceptional teaching fellows—comments that must have meant a great deal to outstanding but still uncertain graduate students cum teaching fellows, many of whom undoubtedly went on to great accomplishments in teaching and research. Here is a sampling:*

- *"...an informed, dedicated, and caring teacher...."*
- *"...conveys to the student (me) some of the joy of scientific discovery...."*
- *"...is able to sit down beside me and explain in simple terms the intricacies of the biological systems we are studying."*
- *"I hope my children encounter teachers like Mr. _____ somewhere in their college careers."*

- *"I have to keep reminding myself of that he is still a stu-dent: He fits my concept of a professional—informed but aware of the inadequacies of that information; enthusias-tic, but not to the point of overselling the available knowledge; and accessible, ready to admit the limitations of his own knowledge."*

A PRIMER ON ETHICS FOR NEW SCIENTISTS

Even those relatively new to science must be con-cerned with the ethical base of their work. Many are ex-posed indirectly as graduate students to ethical problems confronting their mentors or other faculty members. Many will have seen examples of practices on the fringes of proper ethics. Some will have witnessed examples of the positive side—in which proper ethics have been ad-hered to, even at a sacrifice of advancement or good rela-tionships with a few colleagues.

Two examples that could be explored include:

- The "bandwagon syndrome," in which scientists redescribe their proposed work to fit particular funding sources interested in research areas in vogue at the moment (e.g., aquaculture, cancer, genetic engineering), even if they have little in-terest in really modifying their ongoing research programs.
- The "Barnum phenomenon," in which well-meaning but gullible donors or private founda-tions are treated royally, fed proposals of dubious scientific merit, and promised results that will be next to impossible to achieve, by scientists

or university administrators interested in their
money.

Examples of many other practices that could be construed as marginally ethical may be observed by graduate students. Responses by such students, when
evidence of ethical lapses, deceit, or even fraud is observed, should be guided by monumental caution.
Professional reputations are among the most cherished
possessions of scientists, and are also extremely fragile,
so any suggestion of malpractice becomes immediately
a most serious matter. It is worth remembering, too, that
the system of science is a highly conservative one, which
will close ranks against outsiders (and graduate students
are still somewhat in that category) unless absolute proof
of wrongdoing by a member is presented. Even then, it
is often expedient for the establishment to find a scape-
goat, and the low person in the organizational hierarchy
(who else but the graduate student?) is a prime candidate. There is, however, a concept called "the triumph
of principle," which can be of such overriding importance to some graduate students as to motivate them to
take the extreme risks involved in disclosure. If such
motivation exists and prevails, though, counsel from experienced faculty members is an absolute requirement.
This is no game for amateurs.

WHAT THE PERCEPTIVE GRADUATE STUDENT
SHOULD ALREADY KNOW

In doing the research for this chapter, I found many
faculty members who wanted to contribute special items
of advice to graduate students and new scientists. Some

of the offerings seemed slightly extreme, some were too pedestrian, but some seemed worth scribbling on a cocktail napkin or a matchbook cover for eventual inclusion here. These statements were often couched in apologetic terms, as though those offering them felt that most new scientists would already be aware of them—but I'm not convinced that this is so.

Here are a few:

- People who *do* things—publish research results in profusion, write books, present papers, organize meetings—may not always be the very best for their jobs, but they *do* them. Many others are sure that they could do better, but, for whatever reason, they *never do*. Moral: Try it.
- A first departmental seminar may be one of the most traumatic events in a young career. Other than an exhaustive preparation for it, a reasonable approach to the inevitable "discussion" (read inquisition) session, and the desired nondisclosure of ignorance, includes the following admonitions: Don't act cocky or know-it-all, but don't admit gross ignorance on any topic. If necessary, disclaim expertise in specific areas while indicating those areas in which you do have expertise. Say "I don't know" very, very infrequently—no more than once in any presentation, if you can at all avoid it.
- Admittedly, you may be very good and very bright, but you are never entitled to be *pompous*. The first time you hear this or an equivalent term used and suspect that it may be applicable to *you*—go out into any situation in which you are unknown, totally, and see who buys your line

(e.g., writers' conference, singles bar, church social, soup kitchen). Seek out people who have nothing to gain from your good opinion—and push them for evaluations of and reactions to your ideas, attitudes, knowledge, or positions on issues. This can be a chastening experience, to say the least.

- If you elect to join an academic institution, you *must* produce "scholarly works" continuously and abundantly, or else you will be overlooked or rejected for raises, promotions, and tenure, and you will be given greater teaching loads and trivial departmental assignments (e.g., public relations committee, planning committee, buildings and grounds committee) that further reduce the likelihood of scholarly production.

- When you are considering a university position, remember that many departments have faculties sharply divided between the lords and the peons—with the lords handling graduate seminar courses, with abundant research time, and the peons (often the new hires) teaching large undergraduate lab-heavy courses, with little time left over for research. Postdocs shake out at a still lower level, insofar as status is concerned.

- Many university departments have associated but largely independent research institutes—the staffs of which constitute an untenured but privileged class (as long as grant funds are flowing). These "selected ones" quickly lose status, and are even terminated, if grant funds dry up. Be sure you understand fully the terms of your employment.

- Successful people know how and when to jump

on or off research "bandwagons." They seem to know intuitively how to get in on the ground floor and to stay in the forefront of a developing field. They also seem to know when to get off, when a technique is becoming obsolescent. As a former mentor from the Eastern Shore of Maryland once told me, in the quaint idiom of that area, "Don't be on the last train from Pokomoke City—be already established in Baltimore." (I can speak from painful personal experience here, as one of the last to use and to publish results based on a technique in systematic serology that was being replaced rapidly by newer and superficially more sophisticated methods—but I was green and stupid, and nobody warned me in time.)

- Minor, but still important, comments:
  - The departmental administrative staff (and especially secretaries) can be important to you. Establish name and face recognition with them through uncontrived personal contacts.
  - On campus, look people in the eyes; speak to everybody; say "Hello," "Good morning"— even to bearded faculty members, and even if they don't respond.
  - In cafeteria, pub, or other discussion areas, talk to people about *their* research, not *yours*.

GRADUATE STUDENT DILEMMAS— SOME CASE HISTORIES

Innocent, gullible young graduate students sometimes become enmeshed in professional situations that are not of their making and with which they are poorly prepared to cope. Although the *specifics* are normally nonrecurring, some of these events have similar *general* characteristics and are worth considering here. The approach used is to list some case studies of student dilemmas, to propose possible theoretical remedies, then to indicate the real-life outcomes.

Case 1. Mark Bean, an outstanding graduate student in psychology, submitted his thesis and left the campus to take a job for which a Ph.D. was a stated prerequisite. Award of his degree was delayed repeatedly because one thesis committee member did not sign—first because of extended foreign travel, then because he ''simply did not get around to it.'' Officials at the new location (a teaching hospital) were getting uneasy about Mark's lack of the promised degree.

 (Possible actions could include pressure on the committee chairman to take drastic action to obtain the signature, a direct appeal by the student to the errant professor, a direct appeal to the university administration to force the professor to sign or at least to offer some explanation for the delay, or none of the above.)

Case 2. Lester Osgood, another outstanding graduate student, was caught in a personal feud between his major professor and another senior faculty member who despised the major professor. The faculty colleague (a member of the thesis committee) delayed the degree interminably by demanding more and more research before he would approve the thesis.

 (Possible actions could include a request by

the major professor for appointment of an alternate committee member, a direct appeal to the university administration for a formal review of the entire matter, departure without the degree, or none of the above.)

Case 3. Jim Bitterman was a good student and a campus leader who had been accepted as a "special student" because of a weak undergraduate background in science. He passed his graduate courses (some marginally), but failed his qualifying exam.

(Possible actions could include shifting to a terminal master's degree program; attempting to dig himself out by heroic makeup efforts, including undergraduate courses; admitting total defeat and dropping out; or none of the above.)

Case 4. Jill St. Amand was a brilliant student who came to the university with assurances of critical financial aid. Unfortunately, during her second year of graduate work, several major university grants were withdrawn abruptly, resulting in cancellation of a number of assistantships, including Jill's.

(Possible actions could be full expectation that the university would honor its financial commitment, with support for the displaced students from emergency institutional funds; acceptance of the bad situation accompanied by a scramble for an outside job; withdrawal from the university; or none of the above.)

Cases like these, and many similar or dissimilar ones, abound on most campuses, and every graduate student can recite several. Solutions vary in the extreme;

some students operate through channels, expecting "the system" to correct abuses; some students are pushed to take more direct (and often less effective) steps; some students simply disappear, often with lifelong bitterness toward the university and even toward science as an occupation.

In the real-life cases presented, Mark Bean took the extreme step of requesting a leave of absence from his new job to hound the delinquent professor for an *entire week* until he finally signed. Les Osgood left the university without a degree, but enjoyed a long and successful government research career (not, however, without enduring hostility toward a system that had failed him miserably). Jim Bitterman tried a comeback, but failed his qualifying exam again, and dropped out of the program. Jill St. Amand dropped out for the remainder of the academic year, then transferred to a more hospitable university, where she received her Ph.D. with distinction—such that she remained there as a faculty member.

SOCIAL FUNCTIONS—PLEASURES AND PITFALLS

It is almost a truism that for many graduate students, events *outside* the classroom or laboratory can have great influence on their education and future careers. The graduate department is a comfortable microcosm in which to develop all kinds of skills useful or critical to a life in science—including social skills. A surprising number of science majors need all the help they can get in developing such skills.

One of the principal practice fields for this development is the departmental social event, especially receptions after awards ceremonies, cocktail parties for visiting scientists, small-group dinners at faculty residences, or other kinds of group encounters of a nontechnical kind. Perspectives and learning curves can vary among graduate students, postdocs, and junior faculty members—but for all, these events should be stimulating, productive components of the acculturation process in science. They offer opportunities for making and developing potentially important contacts, in what is for some a relaxed environment (for others, though, these events can be highly stress-inducing).

After too many years of casual behavioral research at these functions, I've come up with yet another list of procedures:

- Without doing so obviously, study some of the party activities of individual faculty people—especially the more gregarious ones. Score their good and bad points, but never discuss your scores with them or any of your cohorts—this is a *self*-improvement exercise.
- Graduate students are sometimes asked to help out at faculty social functions—tending bar, registering guests, setting up tables, arranging refreshments, carrying out trash. This too can be a unique learning experience for the observant, if it is done with grace and a smile, and if you stay in the background.
- Social functions may offer opportunities for fleeting contacts with at least some of the ''right people'' in your discipline—but don't expect them to remember your name or what you talked about, since they have their own agendas at such affairs.
- Avoid your friends, except for a brief greeting.

Don't gravitate to a small comfortable circle of co-horts and roost there—mingle, act pushy, ask people about their research.

- Limit alcohol intake to a few weak drinks (but they are usually weak at these affairs, anyway).
- Before the event is over, you should have met most of the participants who are in your field, including the authority figures, but don't try to monopolize the time and attention of the principal actors, unless they encourage your advances. Some get very impatient with overly aggressive juniors.
- During one-on-one discussions, if your companion begins fidgeting or if his eyes wander, terminate the conversation at once—that person is trying to escape from you.
- Often, there will be guests of honor or power figures for whom the reception/party/affair is given. Usually, these people are attended by a faculty member fingered for the job, but they should never be left alone to stand with a plate of hors d'oeuvres or to wander about the room. If the host committee does not provide support, appoint yourself to cover the gap temporarily with some unobtrusive company. Such people, regardless of their professional accomplishments, may feel ill at ease in a room full of strangers and may appreciate your overtures. Approach this situation very cautiously, though, so as not to convey the impression of pushing your way in.

Obviously, this list is only a beginning. Nuances and variants of social behavior are endless, often shaped by individual preferences and aggressiveness. The one constant is that these so-called social events are important to careers in science as well as in other professional occupations, so they should never be underrated or avoided.

CHAPTER 3

HAVE YOU HUGGED YOUR MAJOR PROFESSOR TODAY?

Mentor Relationships for Graduate Students; Training Your Major Professor; Fate of the Orphaned Graduate Student; A Classification Scheme for Major Professors

INTRODUCTION

Chapter 2 dealt all too briefly with some principal issues in graduate student development, but it ignored completely what is undoubtedly the most important personal relationship for incipient professionals—that of mentor and protégé. The subject was treated broadly in the second volume of this trilogy (*The Joy of Science*, Plenum Press, 1985), but it deserves a closer examination from the perspective of the junior partner in the relationship, the graduate student, and that is the objective in this chapter.

Professors (many of them, anyway) are people! True, few of them could be described as "average humans," and all of them have strengths and weaknesses, lovable and hateful traits, and moods reflecting joy or gloom. But most of all, professors have needs—to be accepted as productive scientists by peers and colleagues, to be promoted and to receive tenure, and even to be thought well of as teachers by students, especially graduate students. Some professors would deny the last need with great vigor, but most would place recognition of teaching accomplishments high on their list of career satisfactions.

The role of "teacher" in graduate education is a complex one, requiring much closer personal relationships with students who have become rapidly maturing new scientists. It is no longer enough, at this level, to be an effective lecturer, a writer of introductory textbooks, and a preparer of fair tests and exams. More is expected, and much of that "more" is commitment to shaping the graduate students who will become tomorrow's competitors for research grants, journal space, significant breakthroughs, and transient glory in science.

It is unusual to find a graduate faculty member who does not take seriously this commitment to developing new talent. It is also unusual to find faculty members who feel adequately appreciated by students and former students for their efforts. Why, if recognition of teaching accomplishment is important to graduate faculty members, is it parceled out so stingily? And how can this defect in the system be remedied?

Any reasonable chapter on figurative hugging and other forms of professional intimacy will of course suggest solutions to these and other problems. Appreciation for professional assistance from mentors need not be a scarce commodity among scientists at any level, except for a characteristic reticence on the part of some participants to express it. Sometimes the crush of getting on with a career prevents adequate expression, despite good intentions; sometimes there is fear that expression may be construed as flattery or seeking favor; sometimes there is concern that the expression may be considered naïve or emotional. For whatever reason, much of what could be said as an honest expression of gratitude is not said, thereby denying pleasure to both participants in the mentor–protégé relationship. This is not a rational state of affairs for presumably intelligent people, and it is one that can be corrected easily: *Tell* a mentor that he or she has been important to you. *Risk* being thought emotional or sentimental or "brown-nosing"—if the expression of feeling is genuine. (Parenthetically, tell *colleagues* also, if they give you moments of pleasure and satisfaction in science—if their actions make you feel good about being a professional.)

There are other problems inherent in the delicate mentor–protégé balance that are not so easy to resolve. Of mutual concern in any such relationship is the respective amount of assistance to be offered and accepted by each party. The mentor must ask: "How much direction and supervision should I give students in thesis research? I may suppress natural creativity and stunt potential for future independence of thought if I offer too much oversight. On the other hand, if I intervene too little, the student may flounder around and waste time, or become depressed and leave, or (worst of all) defect to another faculty member ready to hand-carry his students through to a degree."

The student must ask: "How much direction do I want from a mentor?" A common complaint is lack of adequate guidance from major professors. The short-term pragmatic attitude of graduate students is often: ''I want a degree, and I need some direction to help me get it as quickly and efficiently as possible—but this is a critical period for me in learning how to do research, so I can't slight it in any way, and I need to act with at least a modicum of independence.''

TRAINING YOUR MAJOR PROFESSOR

Most students, like most professors, are people, and it is especially important to graduate students that their major professor see them as such. Sifting through the many discussions that form part of the foundation for this book, I have found the expectations to be that the professor will view his graduate students as:

- People with some acquired knowledge, not just students.
- Human beings with lives outside the laboratory, even though graduate studies are a major, if transient, part of those lives.
- Psychologically complex entities, with likes and dislikes, strengths and weaknesses.
- Junior partners in the research endeavor, willing to learn but expecting to bring ideas and independent thinking to the work—beyond that of a technician.
- Eager, if relatively uninformed, participants in any broad discussion of science—philosophical, conceptual, or technical.

Most major professors, on reading this list, would say, ''Of course I do all these things''—even if they don't. How to help them, unobtrusively, to do them, or to do them better, in the middle of normal daily chaos is another graduate student dilemma, to be addressed here.

A moderately astounding fact, which is not appreciated by many graduate students, is that *most professors are trainable*! This applies to faculty members of any age or status, even though the more "mature" ones may have developed some immunity to being manipulated by students and may therefore require more perceptive handling.

It is most important to establish a dialogue with a major professor early, through *brief* discussions, using, as logical entry points, subjects such as required and optional courses as well as research matters. If either member of the partnership—student or professor—is by nature reticent, the discussions may never go beyond these required topics, and that is a mistake! The professor has a fund of experience and insight that should be explored, but may not be unless the student takes some initiative. One of the best and simplest approaches is to come to the discussions with a topic or a short list of topics (assuming that the timing is correct and the professor is not grading exams or in the midst of preparing a technical paper). Subjects that might be proposed include, but are certainly not limited to, ethical behavior in science, activism and advocacy positions taken by scientists, student–faculty relationships, the historical development of the professor's specialty area, journals and publications, techniques in lecturing and seminar presentation, the so-called scientific method and its variations—and on and on through topics of interest and concern to both parties. It will become apparent quickly which areas the professor enjoys most, or at least feels comfortable in discussing, and this insight can be the basis for future meetings. The student can't be just a sponge, though, but must bring to the discussions some thinking and opinions beyond a mere succession of questions.

Another training technique that I have seen used effectively is to ask the professor to participate weekly (or at least on some regular basis) in luncheon, brown bag, or similar small-group discussions (usually limited to his graduate students and postdocs) of some of the broader science-related topics mentioned above. This is *not* the customary brown bag seminar. The conversation should be informal give-and-take, with possibly a rotating student moderator. Such a format serves several purposes: It permits expression of student views on the subject; it leads the professor to examine his own opinions on the matter at hand, beyond mere top-of-the-head comments; and it may lead to subsequent reexamination of positions by all participants (including the professor). None of these "group therapy" approaches, though, is as effective as continuing one-on-one conversations, always at the option of the professor but often at the gentle insistence of the protégé.

The most fortunate graduate students are those able to work as teaching fellows in courses offered by their major professors or as research assistants in his grant-supported studies. These jobs offer superb opportunities for visibility and continuous interaction. For the bright and competent, there are no better routes to a more personal yet professional relationship with a person who has a good piece of any future prospects in his hands.

FATE OF THE ORPHANED GRADUATE STUDENT

The ending of an intimate relationship is never easy. Few associations in science are closer than those of graduate students and major professors; some of them persevere long after the degree is awarded, and most are characterized by mutual respect and often friendship. Occasionally, though, events lead to premature termination of the arrangement. A major professor may accept a position elsewhere, or may retire prematurely because of illness, or may die; a graduate student may be unable, financially, to complete thesis work, or may feel it necessary to enter the family business.

Separation becomes especially acute if the graduate student is left as an orphan in a harsh world because of the sudden disappearance of a mentor. What was projected as an orderly progression toward a degree becomes chaotic, with much scurrying around for a replacement major professor, for a reconstituted thesis committee, for new laboratory space, and even for a changed emphasis in thesis research. The student may have been supported partially by the former mentor's grant, so new financial backing must be located, if it is available at all. The student may become depressed by the apparent collapse of his or her universe and may actually withdraw from graduate school. Usually, though, the separation is like a divorce, with time healing all but the most severe wounds. A new major professor is found, often one just as compatible and knowledgeable as the former one; thesis research resumes with only minor delays, and the student's universe is gradually reconstituted. Sometimes, the change is even beneficial, with new perspectives and directions supplied by the replacement mentor. Only rarely is the change harmful in the long term, regardless of initial predictions.

Graduate students and postdocs who have gone through the process of becoming orphans are almost unanimous in declaring it a traumatic and stressful period in their careers—but one with few if any lasting effects beyond a possible transient delay in thesis completion. Most retained affection for the former mentor, but many found the new relationship to be equally satisfying.

It is worth mentioning that there are instances when graduate students are consigned to the orphanage by a voluntary act of their major professor. Such a traumatic event may be the consequence of severe personality conflict or dissatisfaction with the student's capabilities or rate of progress. For the student, becoming a "free agent" after some period of graduate studies is not a desirable state to be in, especially if his former major professor has been outspoken among colleagues about the reasons for separation. Most graduate schools, however, are tolerant, provided course grades are satisfactory, and a replacement professor may be assigned or may be coerced into volunteering. Sometimes the new relationship is successful, if the conditions that led to the first divorce do not reappear. Fortunately, these events are infrequent; most mentor–protégé unions persevere.

A CLASSIFICATION SCHEME
FOR MAJOR PROFESSORS

This chapter began with the intuitive assertion that professors are people. If this is accepted on faith, at least provisionally, then any attempt to put them into the pigeonholes of a classification scheme should fail. Even so, the average graduate student needs some guidelines for selecting a major professor—some preferably quantitative way of reducing risks of an incorrect or inappropriate choice. Until now, there has been no extensive literature on the subject, but this section outlines a classification and evaluation scheme that should reduce the burden of decision-making for graduate students already overwhelmed by the need to make choices about sex partners, vegetarian diets, dropping out, which sports car to buy, which bank to rob next, and a host of others. The scheme—actually a simplified risk analysis—yields a comforting final number that can be stirred into the pot, along with results of applying other more subjective criteria, as a crutch in the mentor-selection process.

The analytic procedure consists of weighted responses to questions in five categories:

1. Level of accomplishment in specialty area
2. Faculty status
3. Number of years at present institution
4. Amount of professional but nonresearch activity
5. Extent and nature of outside activities not related to science

The complete list of questions is included in Figure 4, together with grading instructions. Note that there is no category headed "Don't know"; if you are tempted to give that response, find out! Note, too, that standard tests for significance should be applied to observed differences in total scores obtained by professors competing for your favor.

Analysis of Professor _____

Category 1. Level of Accomplishment in Specialty
Scoring: high, 3; medium, 2; low, 1.   *Score*
a. Has he/she published several substantive papers
    in the past three years?   _____

b. Does he/she present papers regularly at profes-
    sional society meetings?   _____

c. Is he/she invited to give seminars at other insti-
    tutions?   _____

d. Does he/she give invited/keynote/review papers at
    symposia?   _____

e. Do others in his/her specialty visit/consult/
    phone/meet with him/her?   _____

f. Does he/she have major research grants in effect
    at present?   _____

g. Does he/she spend at least three hours in the lab
    each day?   _____

h. Does he/she subscribe personally to more than
    five professional journals?   _____

i. Has he/she published review papers or books in
    his/her specialty area?   _____

Category 2. Faculty Status
Scoring: high, 3; medium, 2; low, 1.   *Score*
a. Is he/she tenured?   _____

b. If tenured, does he/she hold an endowed chair?   _____

c. Is he/she a member of the faculty senate or com-
    parable faculty organization?   _____

d. Is he/she a member of important academic com-
    mittees (awards, tenure, ethics, other)?   _____

e. Has he/she advanced in rank at a normal rate?   _____

FIGURE 4. Risk-analysis questionnaire for selecting a major professor.

f.　Is most of his/her course load at graduate rather than undergraduate levels?

Category 3.　Number of Years at Present Institution
Scoring: high, 3; medium, 2; low, 1.　　　　　　　　*Score*
a.　Has he/she been at present institution for at least three years?

b.　If a full professor, was this rank achieved rapidly or slowly?

c.　If a long-term faculty member, has he/she been granted sabbaticals?

d.　If a long-term faculty member, has he/she been invited to serve in a visiting capacity at other institutions?

e.　Is he/she more than four years from minimum voluntary retirement age?

f.　If over 50 (or more than 20 years beyond his/her Ph.D.), is he/she physically active and in apparent good health?

Category 4.　Amount of Professional but Nonresearch Activity
Scoring: high, 3; medium, 2; low, 1.　　　　　　　　*Score*
a.　Is he/she a member of the principal professional societies in his/her specialty area?

b.　Does he/she hold office or membership on the board of directors of a scientific society?

c.　Is he/she a member of the editorial board of a national journal?

d.　Does he/she attend national and international conferences?

e.　Does he/she serve on grant review panels for government research funding agencies or foundations?

FIGURE 4. *(Continued)*

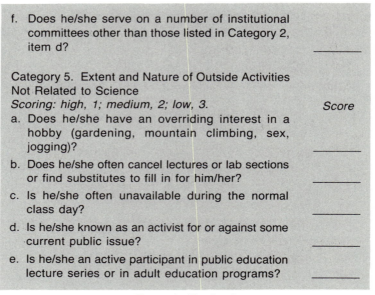

f. Does he/she serve on a number of institutional committees other than those listed in Category 2, item d? _____

Category 5. Extent and Nature of Outside Activities Not Related to Science
Scoring: high, 1; medium, 2; low, 3.   *Score*
a. Does he/she have an overriding interest in a hobby (gardening, mountain climbing, sex, jogging)? _____
b. Does he/she often cancel lectures or lab sections or find substitutes to fill in for him/her? _____
c. Is he/she often unavailable during the normal class day? _____
d. Is he/she known as an activist for or against some current public issue? _____
e. Is he/she an active participant in public education lecture series or in adult education programs? _____

FIGURE 4. *(Continued)*

These objective criteria seem harsh and almost impossible to satisfy, but the high scorers are the ones to be associated with as a graduate student. They are the movers and producers, the leaders in research areas, the participants in significant meetings (to which students might be dragged along), the ones to whom colleagues turn when a good junior position becomes available.

Unfortunately, these criteria are deficient in not considering more personal and hence more subjective ingredients in selection of a major professor—those concerned with *individual rapport*. These critical ingredients can with some effort be manipulated into a roughly quantitative assessment, using the format in Figure 5.

Personal rapport with Professor _____

Scoring: high, 3; medium, 2; low, 1.   *Score*

a. Does he/she really listen to me or slough me off
   after five minutes?   _____

b. Does he/she consider my suggestions without being threatened by them?   _____

c. Does he/she know me as a person, and do I know
   him/her as a person?   _____

d. Does his/her research seem exciting and relevant
   to *my* interests?   _____

e. Does he/she give me a fair share of attention without making me feel I am making undue demands
   on his/her time?   _____

Rapport of Professor _____
with his/her current students

Scoring: high, 3; medium, 2; low, 1.   *Score*

a. Does he/she seem to genuinely enjoy personal
   relationships with graduate students?   _____

b. Does he/she guide without dictating?   _____

c. Does he/she treat students as equal partners in
   a research venture?   _____

d. Does he/she mingle socially with graduate students and postdocs?   _____

e. Does he/she encourage and participate in brown
   bag or similar gatherings of his/her graduate
   students?   _____

FIGURE 5. Risk-analysis questionnaire for assessing rapport of potential major professor with self and others.

These more personal aspects of the selection of a major professor are important, but may not warrant equal rank with the more objective criteria presented earlier. The purpose, after all, is to obtain the best possible graduate education. If this must be done at some sacrifice of a wholly comfortable daily relationship, then let it be so!

It must be emphasized that these semiquantitative analyses are only aids in decision-making; other factors may intrude to modify any final choice of a mentor. Probably the most important of these factors is that the faculty member whom you choose *may not want you as a student,* for reasons such as a current overstock of graduate students, uneasiness about an unimpressive undergraduate record, or instant personal dislike. Beyond this uncontrollable factor, there are others that should enter into the decision process. Early interviews may disclose sharp personality differences that could make a long-term relationship stressful or unproductive. Some professors are noted for requiring more and more research results, so that a thesis is rarely completed. Some professors are thoroughly disliked by a majority of the faculty, and some of this dislike can be transferred to students of that professor. Some professors are so completely engaged in their own research that they have no time or patience for graduate students. Any of these deficiencies may present major problems for innocent graduate students.

So, the choice of a mentor is not an easy one, but it is an important one. Fortunately, it is not immutable. The relationship can be terminated with good cause by frank discussion and a substitute selected—preferably on the basis of greater experience as well as simple questionnaire results.

Before we leave this topic of selection of a mentor/major professor, it might be instructive to look at the flip side—the factors that he might use in deciding for or against your candidacy as a protégé. The decision process will probably be far less formalized than that just proposed for students, but some sample questions that may be important in decision-making include these:

- Does the student have a good, sound undergraduate record in science and mathematics?
- Does the student make a reasonable public appearance—is he reasonably tidy; does he talk logically and in an organized fashion?
- Does the student give evidence of enthusiasm for science, beyond being enthralled by the perceived glamor?
- Does the student give any evidence of reading in the subject-matter area?
- Does the student give evidence of ability to handle equipment efficiently?
- Will the student be able to coexist with cohorts as part of a team in a laboratory environment?
- Does the student appear motivated, with some indications of a high energy level?
- Is the student able to plan and synthesize, as well as merely to absorb factual information?

Faculty people of course search constantly for the ideal student, but usually accept a reasonable compromise, if answers to these questions are mostly positive.

CHAPTER 4

THE SAVVY FEMALE
GRADUATE STUDENT

Relationships with Male Faculty Members; Relationships with Male Cohorts; Sex and the Female Graduate Student; Risk Analysis and Risk Management for Female Graduate Students

INTRODUCTION

In an earlier, simpler era of science—in 1982—I wrote down and actually published everything I thought I knew (one short paragraph) about such absolute crudities as "Sex in the Laboratory," "Rules of Dalliance for Scientific Supervisors," and "Typecasting Female Scientists." These honest but hopelessly naïve attempts to describe the realities of male–female relationships in science were met, understandably, with various overt forms of hostility, ridicule, and humorless laughter from female acquaintances (none of whom allows classification as "friend" since the book was published).

But it was a true learning experience for me, however painful and ego-destroying it may have been at the
time. The quintessence of what I learned is that:

- Males in science have totally erroneous perceptions of females in science—whatever those perceptions are, they are wrong.
- Males cannot treat the vestiges or the actualities of
  sexism or sex discrimination in science with humor, since to most female scientists there is no humor in the subject—nor is there margin for levity
  in the disparate treatment of females in the history
  of science.
- Some female scientists still feel isolated in a male-
  dominated occupation, and they still feel excluded
  from the ''in groups'' that exist.

But good things are happening, and that is the message of this chapter—that females are emerging in increasing numbers, not only *operationally*, as research
scientists and senior faculty members, but also *manageri-*
ally, as administrators and managers of research groups.
The route is still not easy. Women must still survive and
prosper in a frankly male-controlled, highly conservative
system, in which power remains concentrated in a hierarchy of male managers, deans, and executives. Females
may still be treated as sex objects and not as real people or professionals—but with diminishing frequency of
occurrence. To counter these anachronistic obstacles,
women have been objecting openly to any form of discrimination and inserting themselves vigorously into
traditionally   male   networks,   especially   the   ''in
groups''—the ''clubs'' and ''fraternities''—that dominate
the action in any subdiscipline. They are doing this not

only by what I call "pushing the system," being assertive and even aggressive, but also (and most importantly)
by being very good as scientists. This has to be the route
to equal access to promotions, salary increases, travel,
and advanced training—to all the perks and rewards of
a truly superb occupation. *The best place for females to begin pushing the system is in graduate school*, establishing
and revising behavior patterns that will carry through to
professional life.

I propose in this chapter to explore four areas that
are especially critical to female graduate students: (1)
relationships with the faculty, (2) interactions with male
cohorts, (3) sex and the female graduate student, and (4)
risk analysis and risk management. I do so only after
extensive field work, consisting principally of conversations with female graduate students and postdocs—
many of whom were more than willing to talk about
their experiences thus far in science, and a few of
whom seemed actually to be leveling with me, despite
my shaky status as an amateur sociologist and a misin-
terpreter of fantasies. For additional reading and
authoritative points of view on experiences of female
scientists *after* graduate school, I strongly recommend a
book and a review article, both with the title *Women in
Science*; the former is by V. Gornick (Simon and
Schuster, 1983), the latter is by J. R. Cole (*American Scientist* 69:385–391, 1981).

RELATIONSHIPS WITH THE FACULTY

Seemingly endless discussions with female graduate
students have led to one generally held conclusion: that

they *are* still treated differently from male students by *some* male faculty members. This differential does not seem to be aged-related, since the percentages for younger and older male faculty members (small in either case) are substantially similar.

Obviously, the subject of unequal treatment is a complex one, easily influenced by the attitudes and backgrounds of the respondents. Some areas of inequality identified by female students (often based on single events) include:

- Use of moderately offensive terms, such as "girls," "gals," "ladies," or "weaker sex," in classroom discussions or conversations.
- Unwarranted assumptions of inequality in field trip assignments or other activities requiring physical efforts.
- Tendencies to ignore female students in seminar or group discussion courses or to interrupt female students when they are talking.
- Unwelcome references to personal features or attire in group situations.
- Rare instances of "borderline passes" or vague sexist innuendoes in casual conversations.
- Rare instances of arbitrary grouping by sex in laboratory or field experiments.

Another general conclusion, corollary to the foregoing, is that when examples of unequal treatment were brought to the attention of the errant male faculty member, the behavior was corrected at once in most cases, although there was always the stray incorrigible.

The discussions with female graduate students also disclosed a number of additional guidelines for selection of major professors, beyond those described in Chapter 3. Some of them are:

- Test for compatibility before commitment. Take a graduate-level lab course with the person to see how the two of you relate, or sign up as a teaching assistant in one of his courses. This compatibility test is of course useful to male graduate students as well, but is of critical importance to females because of lingering tendencies by some male faculty members to treat female students as technicians, or to view them as interesting *adjuncts* to science, or to ignore them altogether.
- Find out, discreetly, what the candidate major professor's *real* views on women in science are— not his stated public views (this may not be easy to do, since some male faculty members have deliberately developed deep cover identities over the years).

The bottom line, in this matter of relationships of female students with male faculty members, seems to be that much of the former overt discrimination has disappeared, and vestiges can be helped to extinction by performance and by vigorous action to destroy remaining roots.

INTERACTIONS WITH MALE COHORTS

Next to interactions with members of the graduate faculty, much of lasting value in people relationships for incipient female scientists can be derived from daily contacts, associations, discussions, and arguments with other graduate students. Much is made of ''peer–

colleague relationships'' in science, as important aspects of most careers. The basics for such relationships should be acquired in graduate school, and since the professional world out there is, unfortunately, still principally occupied by and controlled by men, the gender connection cannot be ignored.

Discussions with female graduate students lead to the not-so-startling conclusion that they *are* treated differently by male students and that they must spend time and energy learning and then following unwritten rules of conduct beyond those applicable to their male cohorts. It is often difficult for male peers, especially the macho types, to accept females as equals, without a little gentle pressure and occasionally some painfully frank discussions. (Handled with tact by the woman, this can be a learning experience for male graduate students too.)

One of my most productive interviews with a female graduate student was conducted in a small tavern on the edge of a large Eastern university campus. Louise Rittgers was clearly superintelligent and almost frighteningly perceptive, and she had her own guidelines for interacting with male cohorts. Here are a few of them:

- *React strongly but with as much control as possible to any indication that you are being put down because of your sex.*
- *Resist just as strongly and just as pleasantly any overt indication that you are being treated as a sex object and not as an equal.*
- *Find out where and when the informal (and mostly male) discussion groups are held and become an active and persistent participant, even if doing so kills off some of your research time.*

- *Be assertive, but never, never let any male call you that derogatorily without responding strongly.*
- *Make a sincere effort to distinguish between "macho" and "masculine" postures among male cohorts. Differences are sometimes blurred, but definition is clearest in their attitudes toward each other as well as toward women. Today's males seem more sensitive about the rights and privileges of females, but their attitudes, if uncorrected, are sometimes still not too different from those of their fathers.*

So—as another bottom line—the female graduate student *can* survive and prosper in an environment often densely populated by male littermates. To do so, she needs resistance to persistent "little boy" attitudes and assertiveness when the situation calls for it.

SEX AND THE FEMALE GRADUATE STUDENT

Having already concluded that female graduate students are on occasion treated differently from male students, and that some special guidelines apply thereto, I do not think it improper to push the whole matter of sexuality a litte further, to see whether other insights can be gained. In discussions with female students, especially those in the later years of their graduate programs, occasional tidbits of advice and admonition were offered in an admittedly delicate subject-matter area—sexual relationships—after assurance of anonymity were given. Some of them seem debatable, but here they are:

- Seek male company most intensively *outside* your own graduate department.

- Junior faculty members normally come equipped with wives or similar encumbrances; this fact, combined with their customary minimal salaries, makes them unlikely choices for serious conquests.
- Acquiring a professional education is demanding enough without complicating existence with serious emotional involvements.
- Plan a complete metamorphosis at 6 P.M. sharp every day, to keep your developing professional existence from monopolizing the entirety of life.

One area of discussion about sex and the female graduate student that seemed to elicit most reactions concerned *affairs between professionals*. Close proximity in an informal environment such as the laboratory frequently leads to increasingly personal and sometimes sexual relationships between professionals or between professionals and support staff members. These close encounters of a noncelibate kind can be listed among the joys or curses of careers in science—joyous while they last, especially if they are long-term, but less-than-joyous if they involve partners with spouses, or if they terminate too soon, and with bitterness. The environment of the laboratory, which may seem so permissive, can also be very confining for former lovers, and the tension engendered may result in the departure of one or both of the participants in an affair and a slightly stressful atmosphere for bemused bystanders during the descending limb of the relationship.

Much titillating information has been published recently about sexual adventures at managerial and other professional levels of business concerns, and long lists of rules and admonishments can be found in books and magazines aimed at that readership (for a sampling, please read a few issues of *Savvy* magazine for female executives). The counterpart literature on sex in the laboratory is inexplicably very thin and anemic, despite an abundance of good source material. Sex is alive and prospering in university science departments and in other scientific organizations, according to sporadic surveys with marginal reliability, reported with great enthusiasm by casual observers.

RISK ANALYSIS AND RISK MANAGEMENT FOR FEMALE GRADUATE STUDENTS

Risk analysis and risk management should be, but often are not, significant ingredients in decision-making about professional careers. *Risk analysis* includes an examination of the consequences of any action or inaction and of the probability of a particular outcome (such as receiving a promotion, salary increase, or terminal contract). *Risk management* includes selecting and implementing the steps most likely to lead to a desired result, with a plan for optional actions if events and future analyses so indicate. The formal methodology is common in industrial operations, but is carried on only informally in reaching career decisions by scientists (although it is important in their technical studies).

Females in science, because of inequities that still exist, should be particularly familiar with, and should make full use of, these assessment and management techniques in reaching career-modifying decisions. Some of the more critical decisions involve modes of interacting with the male-dominated power structure and with the males who make up that structure. A sampling of these interactions would usually include analyses and decisions about such matters as choices of mentors, about the extent to which being a woman will be allowed to intrude on professional relationships, and about job choices. There follow some examples that illustrate the method:

Marie Cuvier is a second-year graduate student with three potential candidates for major professor: a young and aggressive male Assistant Professor trying to assemble an active research group; a male Associate Professor who has been on the faculty for 15 years and has achieved a modest reputation in his specialty; and a female Associate Professor who has been on the faculty for 20 years and has become somewhat disillusioned about her own status and that of all women in science. Which would be Marie's best choice as a mentor?

Some factors to be considered are:

- *Is the Assistant Professor going to make it, and can I stand the pace of massive doses of science day after day and night after night?*
- *Can I work independently, or would I be more comfortable in a strong mentor relationship?*
- *How important is female equality, in the broad sense, to me as a professional?*

Marie has prepared a table of risks and benefits for each option, considering these and other questions and attempting to weight her responses, but she is still uneasy about the completeness of her assessment—

knowing intuitively that regardless of the choice, it will probably be wrong.

Jeanne Kennedy is a chemistry Ph.D. candidate who has applied for jobs as a junior faculty member at a midsized university, as an assistant chemist in a large pharmaceutical company, and as a grant examiner in a Federal agency. She is good enough to be a serious contender for any of the jobs, but is still uncertain about which way to jump if any offer arrives.

Some factors to be considered are:

- *The present job market for introductory-level university faculty in chemistry is stagnant, and competition eliminates all but the best. Am I among the best?*
- *There is a real danger of becoming a nonentity as a junior research team member in a large Federal laboratory and an even greater danger of disappearing into the middle bureaucracy of a granting agency. Do I want this?*
- *Introductory industrial jobs, especially for women, tend to be at the glorified technician level, regardless of title. Am I ready for such a high-stress environment?*
- *People relationships—not one of my strong points—are important regardless of the job, but are especially important in academic jobs. Can I handle this?*

Jeanne had of course prepared a list of risks and benefits based on these factors and had decided that the industrial job was her lowest option. Then an offer came from the pharmaceutical company, and she accepted it immediately.

These are only examples of the kinds of assessments that should be made, more or less formally, by female scientists; many must include consideration of the effects of gender, regardless of good words about equality. Some risk factors for women are *not* the same as those for men and must be evaluated from different perspectives.

And this, I think, is enough for the moment about the joys and discomforts of female graduate students in science. Certainly much more could be said, and undoubtedly greater insights could be gained, from additional interviews and introspection—preferably by a female inquisitor, or at least by a male–female team. We have touched on some of the sensitive areas—relationships with male faculty members, relationships with male cohorts, sex in graduate education, and assessing risks for females in a still-male-dominated community. The trip, although it has had its disappointments, has revealed a field in which change is finally being realized.

CHAPTER 5

NEW SCIENTISTS ON STAGE: LIVE PERFORMANCES

Presenting Scientific Papers at Society Meetings; Organizing and Presenting Seminars; "Outreach" Activities—Talking to General Audiences; Preparing Lecture Notes; Coping with Visual Equipment

INTRODUCTION

New scientists, including graduate students, are thrust quickly—sometimes before they are ready—into the specialized arenas of their trade, to prosper or flounder, depending on innate and acquired abilities. *Oral presentations* constitute severe tests for most beginners and even for many who are no longer beginners. Scientists do not always need to win prizes in public speaking contests, but they are expected to conduct themselves as professionals in a variety of public forums—whether the forum be a seminar attended by colleagues or an after-dinner talk at the local Rotary Club.

Much has been written about effective oral communication, but scientists usually have little time for such peripheral literature—often to their sorrow and to the detriment of their careers. The hope persists, though, that some stray piece of published advice will capture momentary attention, and it is for this reason that a brief discourse on live performances seems useful here—especially for new scientists. Next to *doing* good science, effectively *communicating* results (oral and written) is most important.

This chapter explores some of the more significant functions of spoken words in science. It offers some advice gleaned from discussions with colleagues who are skilled performers, largely as a consequence of long experience. It even tries to make the point that good oral presentations don't just happen—they are the result of painstaking preparation, constant practice, and study of the performances of others.

PRESENTING SCIENTIFIC PAPERS
AT SOCIETY MEETINGS

Research on any topic in science is incomplete until results and analyses are made known to colleagues, in either oral or written form, or both. Good research demands good presentations of findings, but variability is extreme—particularly in oral presentations, in which effectiveness depends so much on practice and on conscious efforts toward excellence.

The presentation of a scientific paper, especially in a society meeting, is a stylized form of public speaking, with a generally accepted format and a selected, often critical, audience. The usual expectations of good public speaking obtain, but superimposed on them are added requirements of scientific credibility, lucidity of thesis development, and placement of findings in the general context of existing technical information and concepts. This is a large requirement, especially since most research papers must be presented in 10 minutes (rarely more than 20 minutes). Superb oral scientific papers are consequences of good research and continuing attempts at self-improvement in delivery—either independently or through specialized training programs. There are so many admonitions, instructions, guidelines, and cautions about speaking in scientific forums that some professionals try to avoid such commitments altogether. For those who are not frightened into silence, probably the best route to continuing improvement is through close study of the presentations of others—good and bad—with analysis of strong and weak aspects. A special study of outstanding scientific speakers is a subset of this recommendation, applicable particularly to those with fears of persistent mediocrity.

Any listing of guidelines for good oral scientific presentations could easily occupy 50 pages of text. Some seem to have greater value to new scientists, and a sampling of favorites follows:

- Professionals should be able to read an audience and to pitch a talk at just the right level—neither too simple nor too complex (even for a general scientific audience), and with visual material neither too sparse nor too abundant. Most audiences that confront scientists consist of colleagues, scien-

tists from other disciplines, bureaucrats, legislators, public action representatives, concerned
citizens, and extremists—but the *mix* of categories
may be of greatly different proportions depending
on the occasion.

- Professionals feel and project enthusiasm for the
  topic at hand.
- Psychological preparation before the event is
  important—getting ''psyched up'' can improve
  performance markedly. Even more important is
  factual preparation, which demands absolute command of the subject matter. A practice presentation, to eliminate tongue twisters and to time the
  paper, is also valuable, especially if conducted before a small audience of friends willing to give a
  supportive critique on what is said and how it is
  said.
- The structure of the presentation is important to
  participants; it should include a brief historical review, an itemization of major topics to be covered,
  a summary of findings with minimal discussion of
  techniques, and an evaluation of the significance
  of the findings, with a brief recapitulation of major points at the end.
- Most professionals allow adequate time for preparation of good slides and tend to reject any trend
  toward use of crude transparencies (note, though,
  that there is a small cadre of theoretical types who
  make a fetish of developing ideas with just such
  crude handwritten transparencies—which are, or
  quickly become, almost unintelligible to the average member of the audience).

- Most professionals do not give ''slide shows'' when invited to give a paper or seminar, but they do have a few carefully selected and excellent slides as adjuncts to the presentation.
- Many papers have multiple authors, each of whom may have a different speciality and may have made a unique contribution to the research. The oral presentation is usually (but not always) made by the first author; the other authors should be acknowledged, and if at all possible they should be close at hand in the audience, in case the speaker gets out of his/her depth during the discussion period.
- Most professionals make a sincere effort to reduce use of jargon in scientific presentations and to eliminate equations with more than three elements.
- Most professionals dress as such and avoid ''under-dressing'' if they are to perform at the front of the session room. (Note, though, that there is a small cadre of usually very bright junior scientists who appear in jeans and plaid shirts, regardless of the occasion and regardless of their roles.)
- Many professionals spend what seems like an inordinate amount of time preparing for any oral presentation—recognizing the difficulty involved in doing the assignment well. Literally hours of fine tuning are required after the structure and content of the talk are roughed out; included are final selection of choice slides, painstaking review of the progression of ideas and data, reexamina-

tion of the validity of every statement, and careful construction of introduction and conclusions.

- A final word on variability is in order. Regardless of how complete the preparation, some presentations may be superb and others just average—for no good reason, except possibly the phase of the moon, barometric pressure, or minor physiological imbalances. This is a reality that scientists live with—as do actors, priests, politicians, nightclub entertainers, and any others who stand up before audiences.

Good oral presentations are an expected component of professionalism, regardless of individual personality traits. The ability to talk intelligently and well—in every kind of situation from informal discussion of research results to a keynote speech—is a necessary part of the scientist's armamentarium, surpassed only by the need for thorough knowledge of the subject matter and for skill in written presentation of research findings.

SEMINARS: THEIR ORGANIZATION AND PRESENTATION

Few treasured institutions in current science are more ubiquitous or more abused than "the seminar." It is a form of presenting scientific information that has become standard in any scientific organization, large or small. The word "seminar" usually connotes a small gathering of colleagues who listens to, and comment on, an informal progress report from an investigator. But it seems safe to say that of all the so-called seminars I have attended in the past decade, no more than a scant handful really fitted this definition. Most of them were formal presentations of completed research, with minimal time allocated for discussion, usually conducted in a venue more suitable for a lecture. Some of them were nothing but slide shows, with brief interspersed commentary on the slides.

The trend can be reversed, though, but the initiative has to be taken by *seminar organizers*. Part of the existing problem is that the role of seminar leader usually degenerates into a scramble to fill weekly or bimonthly slots in the schedule; to invite, transport, and house speakers; and to locate standbys for the inevitable no-shows. Neither is the job treated with much respect by administrators in awarding course credit for faculty people who accept the organizing assignment. Often, the seminar series is even treated as an extracurricular activity (which it surely is not) by those same administrators. Often, too, more junior members of any scientific group get tagged with the responsibility. The correct perception of the seminar series, and one held by many scientists, is that it is integral to the vitality of the organization and is an important component of the networking system of science.

A principal complaint about seminars, voiced with some consistency by a few in any scientific organization, is that they waste valuable research time, especially if some of the subjects are not immediately related to the narrow interests of those few. Some members of the staff are sufficiently hostile as to boycott the entire series, except for the rare presentations that may happen to be in their specialties. Somehow, the concept of broader communication within a discipline eludes such holdouts; the consequences are apparent in the often poorly populated session rooms and in the obvious lack of interest evinced by some of those who *do* attend. The idea of a seminar series as a *community* activity, to be supported by *all* members of the group, needs to be fostered in some way. One approach to better participation is for the Department Chairman or the Director of the organization to make it clear that all professionals are *expected* to attend and (in graduate departments) to make attendance by students *obligatory*. This seems a little dictatorial, but it is not uncommon. Other approaches are less arbitrary, but are not panaceas; they focus on making the seminar series *better*—even excellent:

- The seminar leader (organizer) should be an aggressive, dynamic, and reasonably gregarious type who is willing to invest the time required to put together a good continuous series. Too often, the job is seen as thankless, a waste of time, and to be avoided.
- The department (or other scientific entity) must have a designated budget to pay per diem, and even an honorarium, to speakers. The amounts do not need to be great, but they should cover expenses.
- The seminar leader should make it perfectly clear well in advance to invited speakers precisely what is expected—especially the degree of informality, the length of the presentation, the nature and numbers of participants, the physical arrangements of the seminar room, the financial arrangements, and even the topics and subtopics that should be covered.

- The seminar should be well advertised, and advance publicity should include not only the speaker's name, affiliation, and title, but also an abstract of the topic(s) to be presented and even a brief curriculum vitae of the speaker.
- Refreshments (at least coffee) should be available before, during, and after the seminar. Too many presentations are scheduled in a bleak classroom, which does little to enhance the pleasure of the event.
- Seminar leaders might even ask selected colleagues to be prepared with brief commentaries on the subject matter of the seminar, in the event that discussion lags (as it often seems to do). Such "designated hitters" could even be encouraged to bring along a few slides or handouts of their own, to augment the presentation. (This needs to be handled very judiciously by the chairman, though, so that the total discussion time is not preempted by a minipaper given by a participant.)

One of the most stimulating seminars that I have participated in recently employed this device of "prepared participants" to good purposes. The seminar topic was an examination of evidence acquired by the speaker from her own research and that of others supporting a somewhat controversial environmental concept. The presentation was excellent, and the speaker clearly indicated the limitations of her data. After the scheduled talk, a faculty member expanded on and differed with some of the conclusions, presenting a few graphs of his own to support a modified point of view. After that, another colleague—a quantitative biologist—got up and gave a brief blackboard summary

*of deficiencies in both the preceding points of view, suggest-
ing additional mathematical approaches. These minipresenta-
tions were followed by more general questions and comments
from others in the audience.*

*The feeling expressed informally by several participants
during the terminal refreshment period was that this was what
seminars should be like but often are not. From my point of
view, it was the added effort by the organizer to identify likely
discussants, and to ask for their participation, that transformed
the seminar from just another ho-hum presentation into a
memorable event. (The quality of the speaker also helped, of
course.)*

- The seminar organizer may act as chairman or may
  ask a colleague who knows the speaker and
  his/her subject matter area to make the introduction and lead the discussion. In either case, some
  preparation is necessary, and some thought
  should be given to introductory remarks that in-
  form and that put all participants at ease.
- Good seminar chairmen guide the discussion with
  great care, encouraging the reticent to be heard,
  gently squelching those with strongly negative
  views, and limiting too-prolonged dialogues
  (usually conducted in jargon) between the speaker
  and some postdoc working in the same field.
- Seminars can be excellent training grounds for in-
  sightful graduate students. Give and take among
  skilled professionals constitutes one of the more
  pleasurable aspects of science (both to the participant and the observer)—an interweaving of so-

cial interplay and technical viewpoints, expressed in an informal but critical environment. Students should participate in these events early and often.
- Seminar organizers should exploit resident faculty/staff members fully, preferably interspersing them with invited speakers, in some rough ratio of three locals to one import.
- Seminars by graduate students near the end of their term are usually expected and often required. Additionally, seminars should be used, more frequently than they are, by faculty and staff as practice sessions for papers to be given at national or international meetings. Feedback from colleagues can improve a presentation or even save it from serious errors or deficiencies.

All these guidelines are oriented toward the seminar organizer as a key figure, and properly so, since he is responsible for much of the success attained. There are, of course, other key figures—the *speakers*—who have their fleeting moments in the sun and who (for an hour at least) can command the attention of a group of colleagues, with profit or loss to both sides. Good seminar speakers, like any group of good professionals, have characteristics that unite them (discounting, as is customary in this book, the outliers):

- Good seminar speakers present their material in a way that invites comment and criticism. This is *not* a time for dogmatism, smugness, or search for approval. It *is* a time for receptivity to suggestions about new or alternative ways of interpreting data, for acknowledgment of perceived gaps in the in-

formation presented, and for appreciation of reasoned comments of peers and colleagues.
- Good seminar speakers are forthright and confident, without being pompous; they are well prepared, but approach the subject matter from the viewpoint of assessing what is known and what is unknown; and they are critical, of their own work as well as that of others.
- Good seminar speakers *enjoy* the opportunity to present results of research and interpretations of findings for the critical examination of other professionals; they listen intently to comments about their work; and they relish the mutual exchange of views involved in the event.
- Good seminar speakers have and convey *perspective* about their research and how it fits a larger pattern of inquiry. They are also generous toward those who have brought understanding of the topic to its current stage.
- Good seminar speakers emphasize the *design of research*, the *progression of thoughts*, and the *emergence of insights*—but do not ignore the false starts and the failed experiments along the way.
- Good seminar speakers try to deemphasize methods and exhaustive treatment of procedures, unless these are integral to the material being presented.
- Good seminar speakers work hard to create a degree of empathy with participants, knowing that this empathy can result in effective (and maybe useful) feedback from the participants on the data and conclusions presented.

The seminar, properly conducted, can be a learning experience for the speaker as well as for the other participants. It provides a forum for testing ideas and interpretations with an informed critical audience. A well-known scientist recently expressed the extreme view that "science has virtually ceased to be self-critical; scientists are non-involved, like the urban populace at the scene of a rape." Such a generalization certainly need not, and usually does not, apply in the seminar environment, where involvement is almost obligatory.

"OUTREACH" ACTIVITIES:
TALKING TO GENERAL AUDIENCES

Scientists in their careers face many types of audiences, from a small group of supportive colleagues in a departmental seminar, to a cosmopolitan audience at an international symposium, to a large evening gathering of the general public. Each audience must be assessed correctly for its interests and existing level of understanding; no two audiences will be exactly the same in background or responsiveness.

Good general presentations of technical material are consequences of the interplay of heredity, temperament, and training, with emphasis on the last. Compared to giving a paper at a society meeting, speaking to nonscientists is more difficult by at least several orders of magnitude. Such presentations, to be effective, must be marvels of organization, clarity, and delivery, accompanied by outstanding visuals. Even though fewer than one fifth of all research scientists actually participate in

public speaking activities beyond a rare appearance before a PTA or local cultural society, those who do more
must carry much of the burden of communication with
the "outside" and therefore must do it well.

A salutary new condition, especially prevalent in the
past decade, is increased awareness of and interest in
scientific matters by all kinds of people. They want to be
informed about the state of science and the advances being made in understanding natural or man-made events.
They want the information, however, in a form that is
condensed, intelligible, and unbiased, and in which relevance to current living is clear.

A less desirable new condition, again with increased
prevalence in the past decade, is the appearance of scientists on programs concerned with public issues of current interest—especially environmental and public health
matters. Meetings may be organized and sponsored by
activist groups, with an overlay of presentations by
professionals. Such meetings need to be approached
with great caution, to avoid being drawn into advocacy
positions. An additional risk is that parts of a scientific
presentation at such a gathering may be taken out of
context by the news media, thereby portraying the scientist as a proponent or opponent of whatever cause is being touted. Still another risk is that of being drawn into
adversary positions with colleagues at public (and non-
professional) forums during meetings conducted by activist groups. The news media, in particular, take great
delight in controversies, especially if they involve professionals. The admonition here is simple: Don't go
into meetings of this kind as an innocent; find out the
nature of the entire program before agreeing to participate; don't let the organizers dictate the type of presen-

tation to be made; and resist with great vigor any attempts to portray you in an advocacy role. This does not mean, of course, that scientists should not have opinions on public issues, but if they are speaking as professionals, their material should be factual and their conclusions should be carefully circumscribed.

A much more innocuous type of public forum, and one that probably constitutes a principal contact point of scientist and nonscientist in today's world, is the weekly, biweekly, or monthly meeting of service groups (Rotary, Kiwanis, Chamber of Commerce, Lions, PTA, Exchange, and others). Program chairmen for those organizations always seem to be desperate for new speakers, especially if meetings are held weekly. Despite their uncomfortable meeting times (usually at an early morning or early evening hour), presentations to service groups can be pleasant, and access is provided to interested if somewhat distracted groups that often include community leaders and other classes of professionals. Make no mistake, though: They expect to be *entertained* as well as *informed*, and they have minimal tolerance for a pedestrian performance. They want to see the relevance of the material to their lives and to public issues, and they expect it to be well packaged in a half-hour (maximum) presentation. Scientists who find themselves on the service club circuit (the word about good speakers is passed quickly from one organization to another) need to consider the informational content of what they present, but they must be effective public speakers as well.

Much of the preceding discussion applies to the research or academic scientist and is less relevant to the "hyphenated scientist"—the scientist-administrator, the scientist-bureaucrat, the scientist-entrepreneur, the scientist-politician, and even the scientist-PR person. For such specialized categories (some colleagues would not even consider them to be within science), public contact is often a principal or even an exclusive job requirement. Quite often, these people are professionals with varying degrees of training, who discovered quite early that they had skills and interests that took them outside the laboratory, or they found out sometime during their careers that research and teaching were inadequate goals, and exploited different capabilities or interests. Some hyphenated scientists established credibility in research before turning to other vocations; some were spirited away or deliberately left research too early to have achieved any great competence or recognition there. Whatever the route to their present positions, these quasi-scientists are, as individuals, usually very clever, people-oriented, energetic, diplomatic, dynamic, and perceptive. They operate in environments that rarely include laboratories or classrooms, yet they are considered scientists by the general public (and they often think of themselves as scientists). Discerning research and academic colleagues recognize the need for these "peripheral professionals" who constitute much of the public interface of science, although they may deplore the sheer *numbers* of "nonpractitioners" in the various hyphenated categories listed earlier.

So the public facade of science, as often represented by individual professionals "on stage," is integral to perceptions of the role of scientists in today's society. The relatively small proportion of the total technical community that is able to interact well with groups of nonscientists should be applauded and encouraged. The messages conveyed must, of course, be correct ones—

that science is an important component of the present-day human experience, that scientists are really human beings, and that the technical advances can be forces for good as well as evil, with the balance heavily weighted on the side of the angels.

PREPARING NOTES FOR A LECTURE

Here and there on this planet, there are a few people with thought processes so highly organized that they can speak beautifully on technical subjects unassisted by outlines, typed notes, or other props. Most of us are not that fortunate; we require and depend on written support material for oral presentations.

A first response to this need—and one that seems superficially logical—is to have the entire presentation typed and to read it word for word. This may ensure technical accuracy, but it absolutely guarantees a deadly dull oral presentation, and to members of the audience, it implies unwillingness of the speaker to make any real effort at effective oral communication. It represents a retreat behind the printed word and is little better than distributing copies of the talk to the audience and standing silently at the podium until everyone has read the material. So please don't read a paper, regardless of the temptation.

One of the worst examples of slavery to typed speeches occurred at a recent workshop, with an invited distinguished evening speaker. For some obscure reason—possibly an attempt by the session organizers to promote an atmosphere of informality—the speaker, the chairman, and assorted dignitaries were assembled on stage, but in chairs arranged around a coffee table. *The speaker, unfortunately, had planned to read his speech, but could not sensibly hunch over his prepared pages laid out on the low table. He picked up the pages and stood up to speak, but of course there was no lectern in sight. He was obviously disturbed; his hands trembled perceptibly; and at one point he dropped several pages of the doomed speech, which of course threw the presentation totally off course while they were reshuffled. Such amateurishness from an outstanding researcher was both embarrassing and regrettable; he had, obviously, much still to learn about professionalism.*

A better alternative is to rough out the entire paper and prepare a detailed key-word outline that will serve as your visual crutch during the oral presentation. The outline can be in typed capital letters, with colored underlining for various levels of organization of the material, and with anecdotes, references to slides, and other notes inserted at appropriate points. The length and detail of the outline will reflect the self-confidence level of the speaker—ranging from a few key words on a matchbook cover or a cocktail napkin to an elaborate typed and annotated near-manuscript. But regardless of the simplicity or complexity of the outline, it is essential to *rehearse the presentation that will spring from it,* since only in this way can its adequacy be tested. If it is too skimpy, then some important information may be overlooked under the stress of the event itself; if it is too detailed, there is a tendency to simply read it (which we have already declared a no-no).

In the end, though, the nature and detail of notes—of visual props for an oral presentation—are matters of individual preference and prior experience. Some speakers cling to 3 by 5 cards, which free them from any dependency on a podium, but which can get dreadfully mixed up if there are too many of them. Some speakers type an outline and then project it (usually in sections) on a screen, as a visual aid for themselves and the audience. This can be effective, if not carried to extremes—such as the speaker simply reading the entire speech from the screen, which smacks a little too much of elementary school. Still other speakers (who, I am convinced, have strong self-destructive tendencies) depend on projected slides as the backbone of their talks. This technique has two major pitfalls: (1) The presentation may easily degenerate into a slide show, consisting of slides presented in rapid sequence (this may be OK in someone's living room, but it is *not* a scientific presentation). (2) The bulb may burn out or the projector may quit, leaving the speaker mute in the dark, unable to move ahead without the vanished visual material. Even after such a catastrophe, though, it is hard to convince some speakers that a *few* well-chosen and excellent slides may be useful *adjuncts* to a talk, but that *projected material must never be in control.*

Special precautions apply to lecture notes for outdoor presentations. The best and cleverest I have seen were notes prepared with waterproof marking pencil on pieces of composition board 1/16th inch thick and fastened together with a binder clip. The speaker had every right to the utmost confidence in these almost indestructible aids—windproof and waterproof—and received

excellent grades for ingenuity as well as approving comments from participants (the content of the talk was good
too).

COPING WITH VISUAL EQUIPMENT

Long ago, in the dim days of "lantern-slide projectors," when large glass-mounted slides were inserted
and projected one by one on a bedsheet hung at the
front of the session room, scientific presentations seemed
more relaxed. Those ancient projectors seemed almost
indestructible and were uncomplicated enough to be
operated by a trained chimpanzee. The greatest mishap
could be the sudden appearance of cracks in the glass
slides because of heat from the lamp or jamming caused
by unfortunate attempts to force slides of nonstandard
size into the simple wooden holders. Today, though, in
an era of beaded screens and complex carousel machines
equipped with independent and malevolent mentalities,
presentations using slides have become tense affairs, in
which both speaker and audience wait with dread for
some abnormality to appear (and it usually does). True
stories about carousel projectors never end, and they
seem to get weirder as new information comes in. Some
recent additions to the lore are these:

---

*At a meeting in a large downtown Atlanta hotel, in one of those
cavernous chandelier-hung ballrooms, the projector's electric-
ity source was connected, unaccountably, to the overhead
lighting, which was equipped with dimmers. Every time the
lights were dimmed, the projected slides also got dimmer, and
they disappeared when the lights were turned out. No electri-*

cian was in sight, of course, and much amateurish scurrying around by bellhops did little good, until a long, long extension cord was located that could connect the projector to an outlet in the hallway—which was independent of the ballroom lighting. This solution worked sporadically throughout the session, with sudden interruptions when people tripped over and disconnected the cord in the corridor.

At a well-known Southeastern university, classroom slide projectors are mounted high on a rear wall (presumably to put the projection path well above the students' heads and also to save space). In normal class use, this plan is awkward but workable, but it fell apart conceptually and operationally when a recent seminar by a visiting scientist had to be rescheduled into a classroom from a larger auditorium. The first hint of disaster was that the projector would move the carousel only in reverse—so the slides had to be removed and reinserted from last to first. The remote control was also inoperative, and no graduate student gofer had been designated as projectionist, so the seminar organizer, a full professor, spent what remained of the hour perched on a folding chair, changing slides manually. Fortunately, the slides were good, but even so, the take-home message for participants—as in so many other instances—had more to do with the errant projector than with the subject matter of the seminar.

Evidence for the truly destructive potential of carousel projectors is so overwhelming, and the total amount of professional time wasted while waiting for amateur repairs in darkened rooms is so awesome, that one foundation, the Wade Institute for Deep Ocean Research of Oxford, Maryland, has just announced a substantial prize, and assurance of a total monopoly market position, to any company that will produce a projector that is absolutely foolproof and amateur-proof. It is a sad commentary on the state of our technology that we can send a camera into space to photograph Saturn's rings, but we seem unable to suppress the time-destroying antics of carousel projectors.

The situation with projectors is serious enough to have inspired the elaboration of a series of dicta, known locally as "Sindermann's Laws of Projection." Followed rigorously, these dicta can do much to reduce, but not to eliminate, the negative impact of equipment malfunction:

- Never, never build a presentation on visual material—especially not on 2 by 2 slides in a carousel projector. To do so exposes you to the risk of enforced silence in a darkened room, with nothing but the frenzied activity of bumblers to amuse your erstwhile audience.
- Carry your own well-tested projector, spare bulbs, long extension cord, screen, and portable electric generator for every talk or seminar in which slides are to be used. Have this standby equipment stacked in the rear of the session room, ready for use.
- If at all possible, slip into the session room early and actually run through your collection of precious slides, to make sure they are right side up and in proper sequence. (This won't always work, though, since the projectionist may be unionized and you may have to turn in your slides the day before the presentation to a technician in a dim basement cubbyhole.)

- For any presentation in which you expect to use projection equipment, always have Plan A and Plan B. Plan B calls for a talk that is *absolutely devoid of any visual crutches* and is to be used after you have stormed out into the audience and pulled the plug on a terrorist projector. Plan B should become operational *early*, at the first tiny sign of an equipment problem.
- For the supercautious speaker, there is an alternative Plan B-1, in which, after the projector plug is pulled, designated assistants (a few of your friends) move quickly through the audience handing out previously prepared xeroxed copies of your most critical illustrations to everyone in the room (in fact, for line drawings, this may be a better method than projecting a transient image on a screen and could do much to reduce permanently the tyranny of projectors).
- From long years of experience with second-hand cars, it has become increasingly apparent to me that machines have feelings and are hypersensitive to hostility emanating from humans. Their response is also humanlike—retaliation. Always spend a few seconds thinking good thoughts about the projector before your paper is announced.

CHAPTER 6

NEW SCIENTISTS OFF CAMERA: PUBLICATIONS

Writing Scientific Manuscripts; Computerized Manuscript Preparation—A Response to the Data Explosion; Reviewing Scientific Manuscripts—A Part of the Mutual Support System of Science

INTRODUCTION

The published record of research findings is an irreplaceable ingredient of science as we know it today. Because of its importance, the record should be concise, precise, and understandable, with results, conclusions, and interpretations clearly identified. Preparation of such contributions to the onward movement of science should therefore be a principal activity of every professional and an integral part of every research project.

Faced with these beautiful, high-minded statements, one can be only surprised and a little disillusioned to find

that much scientific writing must be described as ranging from mediocre to terrible and that effective communication of research results is *not* a major goal for every
professional. Proficiency in writing scientific papers is an
acquired skill, best mastered early in any career. It builds
on competence in spelling, grammar, paragraph construction, and logical presentation of information, which
normally begins in elementary school and progresses
haltingly through secondary school and college. New
scientists bring to their other professional functions such
varied backgrounds of training in writing that significant
efforts are often required on the part of mentors,
reviewers, and editors to ensure that adequate communication levels are attained.

   This chapter skips lightly through some very selected
aspects of the evolution of written contributions to an already overcrowded literature, with the hope that
somewhere—in a tiny office-lab on some remote
campus—a single manuscript in preparation may be improved to some imperceptible degree.

WRITING SCIENTIFIC MANUSCRIPTS

   Just as oral presentations of research results at
professional society meetings are part of the stylized, almost ritualistic structure of current science, so too are
written papers reporting results of research—papers submitted to specialized journals for publication. The format for such papers is rigid, designed to present, in a
seemingly logical sequence: (1) the problem to be approached and its background, (2) the design of the study,

(3) methods used, (4) results obtained, and (5) discussion of results as related to the findings of others. Brevity, precise language, adequate statistical tests, concise tabular presentation of data, and sparse but highly informative illustrations are all desirable attributes.

With such seeming inflexibility, one would think that most scientific papers are uniform, standard, and of average dullness. One would be wrong. Some papers are examples of beautiful expository writing, encased within the prescribed format, while some are hopelessly obscure and imprecise, even though they may follow that same format. The elements that separate the best manuscripts from the poorest include the design and execution of the research plan, the significance of results obtained, and the writing skills used in reporting the results.

After scrutinizing literally thousands of manuscripts, ranging from the superb to the deplorable, I find it possible to perceive sources of strengths and weaknesses in all sections of the documents. As might be expected, from all this reading and weeping has come a flood of suggestions, admonitions, and dicta that may be useful to beginning scientists—in that they may help them avoid the twin traumas of harsh criticism and rejection. It would seem sensible in offering these comments to march grimly from one standard section to the next, casting pearls and epithets along the way.

1. *Title*. Readers have every right to expect a title that describes the content of the paper. Unfortunately, this is not always feasible if the title is to be kept reasonably short (as it should be for referencing purposes). Brevity, however, invites

abuses of syntax that may yield comical results; brevity may also lead to misconceptions about the content of the paper, resulting in loss of readership. The construction of a title deserves attention; it may easily determine whether the paper will be read by colleagues. Since most scientific writing is a somber business, catchy titles such as those used for many works of fiction are, unfortunately, out of place, even though the temptation to try one may be great (how about such titles as "Stable environmental requirements for seahorses" or "Worms, germs, and maladies of sperm whales"?).

2. *Abstract*. Most journals now publish, in tiny, almost unreadable type, an abstract at the beginning of the paper. As can be deduced from its name, this section should abstract the *essence* of the paper in a brief form for the journal skimmers or for those who may be undecided about reading the whole paper. Since this short section may be the only part of the paper ever read by most colleagues, it should be executed with great care. It should emphasize the objective(s), the research plan, and significant findings, and deemphasize techniques or the work of others. It should *not* (as many do) merely describe what the paper is about or make general references to what will be discovered in later sections. It would be well if it could be printed in bold type rather than in miniature, but this is a matter of style for journal editors.

3. *Introduction*. Some authors say too much and others too little in introducing a paper. The ideal

would be a brief description of the problem to be approached and a short summary of the status of knowledge—followed by a statement of objectives and research plan. The introduction is not the place for an exhaustive literature review; it is the place to describe exactly what the paper is about.

4. *Methods.* Many authors make a hash of this section. They may describe in great and unnecessary detail the excruciating minutiae of techniques, or they may simply refer to methods described in other papers—either of which is unsatisfactory. A good rule of thumb could be that enough information should be provided to enable a colleague to replicate the work, if he/she were so inclined (even though this seems to be a vanishing practice in most areas of modern science). If detailed statistical tests are performed, this is the place to describe them, unless derivation of models is a part of findings to be reported.

5. *Results.* This section is the core of any paper and should be a lucid, straightforward presentation of findings unclouded by discussion of the significance of the results or relevance to findings of others. If graphs or tables are included, they should be described and considered and not be left as unidentified orphans in the middle of a page. If illustrations are used (photographs, for example), they too should be described.

6. *Discussion.* This section provides the only real elbow room for the author, but the privilege must be used judiciously. The discussion should concentrate on placing the results being reported

within a larger framework, by comparison with other published literature and by elaborating on the significance of the findings. It is not a place for poorly supported speculations or for an extended literature review. It should derive its structure from that used in the "Results" section, and its length should not exceed one fifth of the total text material.

7. *Conclusions.* Many scientific reports trail off with a discussion of findings, occasionally with a terminal sentence or two of generalizations. A much better structure (subject of course to the whims of the journal editor) is to create a separate section headed "Conclusions" in which the author's assessment of the findings can be presented in a paragraph or a page. This section should be more than a restatement of results and less than a summary of the discussion. It is not easy to prepare, but it does bring the paper to a more satisfying end point.

8. *Acknowledgments.* Many people contribute to the research reported in a scientific paper; few of them can be squeezed into the list of authors. It costs little, and accomplishes much, if people who applied significant efforts to the work are identified, together with the nature of their roles. Such acknowledgments should not be effusive and obviously cannot and should not include all who assisted in a minor or routine way, in accord with their normal job assignments. Key words here seem to be "reasonable generosity" on the part of the author(s).

9. *Literature Cited.* On rare occasions, a colleague may be interested in some of the published information in the specialized area being reported and may turn to the references cited. Citations should therefore be complete, accurate, relevant, and in quantity adequate to demonstrate that the author is aware of the status of research in his/her field. It is *not* ill-mannered to cite your own papers, provided they are pertinent to the subject of the paper and provided these citations do not number more than one tenth of the references in the section. It *is* poor form to deliberately and obviously ignore significant related papers published by a colleague whom you dislike or by serious competitors in the priority game.

Much of the foregoing discussion seems to concern writing skill—which indeed it does. Not to be obscured, however, is the basic requirement of *good science* on which to base a well-written paper. The ''silk purse'' concept applies here: Poor or mediocre science will remain so, regardless of how elaborately it is presented. The converse is not true, though—good science can be and should be materially enhanced by good written presentation.

Manuscripts receive final scrutiny within a system of reviews of manuscripts before and/or after submission to journals. Good reviewers may point out incomprehensible sentences or paragraphs, major errors in syntax, repetition of words, excessive use of jargon, or other grammatical abuses—even though their primary role is assessment of the *science* on which the paper is based.

COMPUTERIZED MANUSCRIPT PREPARATION:
A RESPONSE TO THE DATA EXPLOSION

Increasingly unable to cope with the flood of new scientific papers, scientists retreat to narrower and narrower specialty zones, where they can comfortably claim that they are "on top of" what is going on in their field. While this course of action is ego-preserving, it plays directly into the hands of those who claim that by failing to stay current in a broader discipline because of the physical impossibility of reading an adequate portion of the literature, *scientists are becoming more and more ignorant* (if ignorance can be defined as a low ratio of what an individual knows to what is available to be known). This thesis was explored recently by George A. Bartholomew (1986). Bartholomew's point seems well taken, yet there is a vague gut feeling on my part that we are not all that ignorant, but that the world is forcing us to become microspecialists, or minimicrospecialists, as a logical consequence of the obvious deluge of new information. One of the best illustrations of this trend is that few scientists *write* books today; they *edit* books, in part because not many professionals feel comfortable enough with an entire subdiscipline to write a book about it. Editing a book, with contributions from many microspecialists—ah, that is easier to live with, and so much less demanding.

But there is a partial solution: *automation* of data summarization, literature review, and even data analysis for manuscript preparation. Some elements of this emerging phenomenon are already operational. Every graduate student knows about (or should know about) computerized literature searches on almost any topic in science and about the availability of specialized abstracting services, once appropriate key words are fed to machines.

What is less widely known, even among practicing scientists, is a recent development in manuscript preparation. An astonishing proportion of scientists have writing blocks of various kinds—induced or exacerbated by harsh reviewers, by kindergarten teachers, by supervisors, or by mothers. For those most seriously afflicted, an extraordinary cure exists that can be described as "formula writing" or "programmed writing." It depends only on access to a modern word processor that has been programmed to select from a number of coded choices in preparing each section and subsection of a manuscript. The paper is constructed by selection from a series of preprogrammed alternative words, phrases, and sentences for each paragraph of a scientific paper— section by section. This procedure is much like preparing preprogrammed form letters that can be constructed paragraph by paragraph. Each type of paper—survey, experimental, ecosystems—would have its own series of programs.

With this approach, the structure of a paper emerges automatically—needing only assignment of a title, insertion of data, addition of acknowledgments, and minor editorial changes to suit individual styles. To illustrate the method, there follows a sampling of some of the programmed elements for each major section of a scientific paper.

Introduction

- Always include in the first paragraph of the introduction one of the following phrases: "There have been few investigations of...," "There is little published literature on...," or "Data are remarkably incomplete on...." Such a statement establishes you instantly as a pioneer and a trailblazer.

- In the second paragraph of the introduction, gently dismiss as obviously trivial the published work of others, with catchy belittling phrases such as "Preliminary findings of Sauerwein (1980)..." or "Earlier exploratory work of Sauerwein (1980)...." Any of these phrases suggests that what has gone before is of small consequence, and yours is the definitive study.

- In the third paragraph of the introduction, make it clear that you are proposing a new concept or synthesis, without actually claiming to be the originator and without ever fully defining the concept.

- In the fourth paragraph of the introduction, make unmistakable but nonspecific allusions to the fact that your approach is innovative, clever, and sophisticated—even if it is routine, mundane, and plodding.

- In the fifth paragraph of the introduction, make occasional but not too obtrusive reference to significant unpublished data that are still in your possession but are not to be revealed in their entirety until some vague later date, if at all.

Methods

- In the first paragraph of the methods section, refer to techniques and/or sampling procedures about which you have previously published, but give only a brief, unhelpful account of them. This will automatically establish your undoubtedly significant role in developing the research area and will force the reader to look (sometimes vainly) for your earlier paper (preferably published as an obscure technical report of a funding agency or still "in press") if he or she wants to evaluate the present paper.

- In the second paragraph of the methods section, present several complex formulas for statistical treatment of data—new derivations—without their developmental steps. Most readers will skip quickly over these, but they will be impressed; the few who might want to evaluate the proposed statistical treatments will be totally baffled by inadequate description of their derivations.
- In the third paragraph of the methods section, propose an entirely new terminology for standard phenomena or for stages in a process—complete with your own definitions. Later use of the terms or categories in your results section should make almost impossible any comparison with the published work of others.

Results

- The first paragraph of the results section must make use of your new terms or categories, describing your findings as unique and different from those of others. This device will keep readers off balance for the entire section.
- Early in the results section, several long, complex tables of data should be inserted. Column head-

ings should be impressive but noninformative, and the tables should lack enough basic data, such as numbers of individuals examined or tested, to prevent meaningful interpretation.

- With this judicious lack of vital tabular information, you are perfectly free in the second paragraph to summarize experimental results as you wish—always with careful statements of the level of significance and adequacy of sample size.

- Late in the results section, a series of complex graphs should be inserted. Those of choice include a mass of data points through which a completely arbitrary curve has been drawn or a family of derived curves with no relation to real data or to the experimental parameters.

Discussion

- The first paragraph of every discussion should reemphasize the important conceptual advances and the generic significance of the reported work. A selection of several of the following words must appear in this paragraph: "concept [conceptual]," "insights," "synthesis," "generic," "analyses of complex variables."

- The second paragraph of the discussion section should cast the results of the study, however trivial, in the broader framework of solutions to fundamental and persistent problems in the scientific discipline.

- Subsequent paragraphs should explore areas of disagreement with the results of others, making sure that the present work is seen as a closer approximation of reality.

- Later paragraphs should rationalize deficiencies in data or anomalous results, making sure that these are suitably minimized and thereby shortcutting negative comments from reviewers.
- A concluding paragraph should consist of resounding but vague generalizations, supported only marginally by results contained in the paper.

Using this programmed or formula writing, every manuscript can be a masterpiece, invulnerable to assault by reviewers, attractive to journal editors, esthetically pleasing to casual readers, and—most important—simple to prepare, even by those with terminal cases of writing block.

Try it. You'll like it! It works! One small private and hypothetical company is now beginning to produce and market tapes with prepared alternative sentences and paragraphs for each section of a scientific paper. The company, Autosci, Inc., will soon be able to provide, at a price, tapes and user's handbooks for all types of scientific manuscripts.

Future directions for "programmed writing" are also emerging. Being tested are systems of computer-produced *entire papers*, requiring only the insertion of data into the program. These papers can then be reviewed by other machines for proper format, use of appropriate key words, and correct application of formula terminology; they can then be abstracted and accessioned by computerized bibliographic data centers, *without ever being read by a human being*. At the moment, though, a principal hangup is in methods to achieve the syntheses necessary to produce good review papers by computer. This seems to be just beyond the current state of the art, despite Autosci's pioneering work in programmed writing.*

If all the preceding seems a tad too mechanical and cynical, one should be reminded here that any astute scientist knows that somewhere in all this automation, the human mind must intrude. Despite increasing dependence on computers, preparation of outstanding manuscripts is to many practitioners still an art form, not to be surrendered totally to machines. Examples of the art intermingled with the science exist, in the exquisitely crafted scientific papers that appear (all too rarely) in professional journals. Lucid, logical, and structurally perfect, they present good science in a form that is not only readable, but also a joy to examine.

Those who persist in preparing, often by what might be considered obsolescent methods, professional papers of gem quality, when queried about their talents and products, have offered these guidelines:

- The science on which the manuscript is based must be impeccable; inadequate or sloppily planned research seldom results in data that can be massaged or manipulated into anything but a paper that transmits the deficiencies.

*Other organizations are of course very interested in programmed writing. According to a recent news release, two mathematicians at Bell Laboratories, Howell, New Jersey, have reported on a two-year programming effort that will revise manuscripts, finding misused words, even sexist words. The machine will suggest better choices for overused or incorrectly used words and even give nonsexist alternative words for the ''no-no's.''

- In rapidly expanding, hence highly competitive, research areas, strong temptations to rush into print should be resisted vigorously, even at the expense of losing some priority. Quality is always enhanced by more-than-adequate data and by at least a few days of quiet contemplation of research results before the word processor keyboard is approached.
- The paper must have historical perspective, preferably summarized in the introduction and expanded upon in the discussion of findings. To do this well, much more of the background and contemporary literature in the research area should be read than would be expected.
- *Results* of research should not be intermingled with *discussions* of those results or *conclusions* drawn therefrom. Furthermore, and probably more important, professionals should be conservative about conclusions and downright reactionary about speculations.
- Drafts of manuscripts should be placed gently in the hands of caring but knowledgeable colleagues for some frank comments long before the definitive draft is typed. Feedback from this jury must be considered very carefully.

So, if there is any conclusion here, it might be that all available mechanical aids to manuscript preparation should be seized and assimilated, but in the end they are only devices and will never supplant the application of an informed intellect to the problem of effective scientific communication.

REVIEWING SCIENTIFIC MANUSCRIPTS

Once a professional scientist has prepared a manuscript for publication, he normally sends it out for examination by reviewers. This is an important networking and support activity, more common in some disciplines than in others but still widespread. It constitutes part of the self-regulating and self-policing system of science, in which colleagues try to protect an author from error, embarrassment, or mediocrity by suggesting changes in the soon-to-be-published document.

Reviews of scientific manuscripts can occur at several levels:

1. Informal reviews of drafts by colleagues who are also friends—usually done at the request of the author.
2. More formal reviews by colleagues who are not necessarily friendly, usually at the request of the laboratory director or other institutional head (such reviews may also be conducted by in-house editors and may include examination for adherence to agency or company policy).
3. Formal reviews by members of editorial boards of journals or by other designated reviewers (also called referees) at the request of journal editors.

Reviews at level (1) are optional, with the author retaining the prerogative of accepting or rejecting the comments or advice offered. At this level, the review process has some similarities to activities of "support groups" of novelists or short story writers, who exchange "pieces" with other members of the group for comments (frequently, but by no means always, positive and supportive). Reviews at levels (2) and (3) may be more binding. Journal editors, for example, tend to heed reviewers'/referees' advice about acceptance or rejection of manuscripts and about the need for revisions. Institutional heads can prevent publication, acting on the advice of in-house editors or reviewers (a practice not uncommon in industrial research and development organizations).

Since manuscript reviews are such an integral part of the support system of science, and since even introductory-level scientists are expected to participate, some guidelines are surely in order:

- A critical question that should be foremost in any reviewer's mind is: "Does the manuscript report good (or at least acceptable) science?" If it does, then advice and comments should concern how to improve the presentation; if it does not, then advice to the editor or other authority figure should be to reject it.
- Reviewers can preserve the author's ego by saying something positive first, before making any really critical comments (provided, of course, that there is something positive to say).
- Reviewers must remember that a big chunk of the author's self-esteem as a professional is wrapped up in any scientific manuscript—so any tampering with it must be done very gently. To some authors, every word is a precious artifact, to be defended stubbornly and enshrined without change on the printed page.
- A temptation exists in reviewing to lean hard on poorly prepared manuscripts. That urge should be

resisted; reviews should always be objective and constructive, never nasty or abusive. Mean or hostile reviews, after initial trauma to the author, may remain dormant for a while (sometimes for years), but will never be forgotten. Retaliation can be sweet in science, as anywhere else.

- A review should be undertaken from the perspective that this is the work of a colleague—who, in some instances, clearly needs help.
- Some journals state the criteria on which a manuscript should be judged; some editors even prepare evaluation sheets with a checkoff system for easy reviewing. High on any such lists are quantity and significance of new information, appropriateness of statistical treatment, validity of conclusions, and clarity of writing. Subsidiary but not unimportant items are adequacy and necessity of illustrations, relevance of discussion section, and suitability of historical framework.
- Authors should learn the important lesson that reviews, even the negative ones, are *gifts*, representing the time and experience of the reviewer (even if he is anonymous, as most journal reviewers are). Comments should be considered seriously, even if the situation is such that their acceptance or dismissal rests with the author.
- Authors should remember, too, that once a paper is in print, it can't be withdrawn or changed. Any errors or misconceptions will remain in that document for as long as the journal exists and will haunt the author for his entire career. Speaking

from my own experience, and that of many professionals, it is much better to know early if something is wrong with a manuscript and to be informed of it—even harshly if that is necessary to get the author's attention.

The discussion thus far has concerned reviews of manuscripts prior to publication. There is a final type of review, not at all unique to science, that can be described as a "public" review, which is often published in news-oriented journals such as *Nature* or *Science* and normally restricted to books. It suffers from the principal shortcoming of any book review—it appears *after* the document is published and is thus not useful to the author, except for ego inflation or deflation. Public reviews may serve other purposes, such as selling copies of the book, but they cannot improve or change what is already published.

CHAPTER 7

SMALL-GROUP ACTIVITIES FOR NEW SCIENTISTS: PAPER SESSIONS, STUDY PANELS, AND COMMITTEES

Participating in Study Panel, Working Group, and Committee Meetings; Convening and Chairing Scientific Groups— Society and Symposium Sessions, Workshops, and Technical Committees

INTRODUCTION

Of the many pleasurable aspects of a career in science, few offer more joy than close working relationships with competent colleagues. Whether in scientific sessions, workshops, committee meetings, or study panel discussions, the various structured exchanges among professionals provide learning experiences as well as occasions for tangible contributions to the support systems of science. It seems important, therefore, that new scientists become informed participants in the many small-group events that are constant features of the margins of any discipline. As is true of other scientific activities with strong interpersonal components, rules of conduct exist and usually prevail, even though they are not immutable.

Extensive personal observations, and discussions with good colleagues, have produced a modest collection of opinions, ideas, and conclusions about how scientists interact in the small-group milieu. With the thesis that such a collection might be useful to new scientists, some of the good stuff has been skimmed off and summarized in this chapter. The orientation is a dual one—to the new scientist first as a *participant* in structured committee and panel meetings and then as a *leader* of such assemblages, as well as scientific sessions. This is an exquisitely complex topic, with nuances important to careers and to the full enjoyment of joint activities with peers and colleagues.

PARTICIPATING IN STUDY PANEL AND COMMITTEE MEETINGS

The lot of a new scientist is never an easy one—with pressures to produce, to publish, to join societies, to prepare lectures, and to get on well with colleagues. Superimposed on all these responsibilities are assignments that seem to be on the periphery of science but are important to careers. Among them is participation in study panels (working groups) and committees—a great consumer of time, but a source of pleasure and visibility to upwardly mobile professionals.

Any attempt to categorize these groups is hopeless, but they have the common image of colleagues gathered around a table to apply their perceptions, expertise, and thinking to a problem that is somehow significant to the onrush of science. Meetings of this kind can provide valuable learning experiences for newcomers. Each participant risks or encourages exposure of attitudes and competencies; each assumes a role in the proceedings; each contributes in some way to the success or failure of the group effort. Learning and contributing must occur simultaneously; observing the performance of good players should be closely coupled with assimilating rules of conduct and performing in accordance with those rules.

Comportment in small-group activities of this kind has been explored by psychologists and sociologists, especially from the group dynamics viewpoint. Since practitioners in other disciplines rarely read very deeply in the jargon-cluttered literature of these two specialties, the following summary of some of the more practical findings relevant to working group and committee participation might serve a purpose, especially for junior members:

- Whatever group you are with, make a meaningful contribution or don't participate at all. "Meaningful" equates with contributions to the discussion that the rapporteur writes down, contributions to the flow of discussion that are useful and not merely distractions, and contributions to ideas and concept development.
- An absolute "must," if the group is of any size, is achieving *positive* name and face recognition; a

real danger is engendering *negative* recognition for what you say or don't say.

- Do more homework for the meeting than might be expected, and give some indication of the extent of your preparation with a few well-chosen and relevant statements early in the session.
- Insert unobtrusive humor if the time and the mood of the group seem to warrant it, but don't become the court jester.
- In entering the flow of conversation, try to relate your comments to what has gone before, and avoid nonsequiturs at all costs.
- Use correct, well-chosen English, free of ''y'know's,'' ''OK's,'' endless sentences, dogmatism, and pomposities.
- Appear for the event in suitable and impeccable clothing, remembering that informality is expected in some (but not all) committee meetings.
- The utmost in good manners is expected of all participants. While the rules of procedure may be less formal than in diplomatic meetings or legislative sessions, courtesy toward other members of the group is an absolute requirement.
- In almost any group, a few members tend to dominate the discussion. A good chairman will take gentle steps to squelch such behavior, but an inexperienced one may not. Occasionally, the situation gets to a point where some more senior member may, during the coffee break, suggest as tactfully as possible that the offender(s) back off a little. Make certain that you are not one of the offenders, but retain your first amendment rights.

- Occasionally, the chairman of a working group or committee may exhibit dictatorial tendencies, which may take the form of attempts to force conclusions or recommendations that are not in accord with the preceding discussion. A perfectly legitimate response to such "railroading" is to ask politely for a review of the rapporteur's notes on the topic and for further discussion to see whether consensus really exists.
- Occasionally, too, the agenda slips enough so that items near the end of it don't receive adequate consideration. If this happens, members of the group can request that any action on those items be deferred or tabled until a later date (if any).

As is the case with most interpersonal relationships in science, the range of variability seen in working groups and committees is broad. The ideal is a session chaired masterfully, with significant contributions by all participants, with stimulating discussion, with the execution of a well-planned agenda—all leading to a report containing conclusions and recommendations that reflect the thinking of the group as a whole. That is the ideal, and being part of the kind of effort that produces it can be one of the genuine pleasures of science.

CONVENING AND CHAIRING SCIENTIFIC-GROUP ACTIVITIES

One of my interests in writing this book is to characterize the "emerging professional"; in fact, the entire trilogy is really about aspects of professionalism in science. My searches for a prototype of the professional—if such exists—have frequently terminated with a subcategory best described as "the chairperson." Members of this elite group are bright and aggressive and rise quickly to positions of power and control in any group. They always contribute to the action significantly and are able to form cohesive groups from otherwise disparate aggregations of individuals.

Leadership positions in science are often less clearly defined than they are in other occupations, so some of the key roles—such as session and committee chairmanships—are more dependent on credibility and group approval than on appointed authority. This distinction makes useful a special examination of the art and practice of chairing scientific sessions and scientific committees.

Scientific session chairmen occupy extremely transient positions with little power, but they can contribute substantially to the success or failure (or the dull mediocrity) of a professional meeting. Minimally, their role is to introduce the speakers, maintain a time schedule, and control discussion after presentations. For those who take the job seriously, though, a host of additional responsibilities are inherent, including:

- Preliminary discussions with session speakers, to get some background on each one and to orient them to the overall objectives of the session.
- Preliminary examination of physical features of the session room—particularly light, microphone, and projector controls.
- A brief preliminary meeting with all participants, just before the session, to count noses, to in-

troduce all of them to one another, and to reduce tension a little.

- A well-prepared introduction to the session, making clear what the objective is (assuming that the session has an objective and is not merely an arbitrary aggregation of contributed papers).
- A brief but relevant introduction of each speaker, stating with great clarity name(s) of author(s), affiliation(s), and title of the paper; if time permits, additional relevant information can be added.
- Light-handed guidance of the discussion that should follow each paper; the awkward silence that often follows the average paper can be broken by one or more questions from the chairman.
- A crisp summary of the session following the last paper; no session should be allowed to dribble off with only a perfunctory thanks by the chairman to the participants.

Other kinds of scientific forums, such as symposia with invited papers, call for much greater exertions by the convener/chairman. For these events, participation begins early, with invitations to speakers that contain detailed descriptions of the purposes of the meeting and the session, with clear statements of what subject matter is to be covered by each speaker, with requests for delivery of abstracts and complete manuscripts by specific dates, with clear indication of the reimbursement (or apology for its absence if there is to be none), with appeals for excellent visuals, and with requests for current but brief résumés.

Symposium participants should definitely be called together by the chairman for a preliminary meeting, preferably in a bar the night before the session or at a luncheon paid for by the chairman (out of his own pocket if necessary). At such an informal gathering, each paper should be reviewed briefly, to be sure there are no serious duplications and to reinforce time limitations. Mostly, though, this preliminary meeting is to acquaint the speakers with one another, to form a cohesive if transient group engaged in a joint effort, rather than just an ephemeral consortium of strangers. This small ice-breaking step can add significantly to the pleasure of the event for all concerned.

Symposium papers are usually published as a group, often in a hardcover volume, with the chairman (as you might expect) responsible for the editing and correspondence with authors and publishers. The job can take on appreciable proportions if it is done conscientiously, especially if some of the papers, after outside reviews, require extensive modifications by reluctant authors. Some diplomacy is required, to ensure that not even one resistant author withdraws, thereby endangering the integrity of the projected volume.

Beyond these more formal roles in chairing scientific sessions and symposia, professionals may be involved in heading study panels, workshops, working groups, or other kinds of technical committees. For these, an additional battery of skills becomes necessary, if the job is to be done with distinction. Most of us have participated in the deliberations of a smoothly orchestrated group effort in this category, but few of us have tried to sort out the factors that lead to success in chairing it. We should. These well-managed events can be intense learning experiences—for the *methodology* involved, as well as for the *nature and excellence of the product*.

During a scientific committee or working group session that is handled well by an astute, experienced professional, many activities take place almost simultaneously, or at least as part of a logical progression:

- The chairman will have selected, insofar as his authority permits, a compatible, knowledgeable cadre of participants.
- The chairman will have appointed a critical consort—the rapporteur—who will be responsible ultimately for much of the quality of the report (and no session exists unless and until a report is prepared).
- The chairman will introduce the objective(s) of the meeting succinctly and will discuss guidelines for conduct of the session, entertaining any dissent at that time.
- The chairman will set the proper tone of the meeting by inserting occasional touches of humor—light and inoffensive comments—indicating that although the objective is a serious one, it need not be reached somberly.
- The chairman will have a prepared agenda, with a provisional timetable that will ensure adequate opportunity for developing conclusions or recommendations (decisions are rarely expected of such groups).
- The chairman will ensure that all participants, even the more reticent, are heard, and will be remarkably intolerant of any action that creates discomfort or injury for anyone.
- The chairman will not allow discussion on any

topic to drift on interminably, nor will he/she cut short what seems to be a productive exchange.

- If a controversial issue is considered at length without resolution, the chairman will call for a coffee break, even if there is no coffee available. Magic often occurs in small-group discussions conducted during such breaks—with prompt solution to what had seemed like an impasse.
- If the committee action on an issue seems controversial, the chairman will make it tentative, to be reopened for further discussion of alternatives at the next session of the group. The morning light often brings sparkling clarity to previously cloudy issues.
- If prolonged discussion among committee members fails to resolve a problem and if tempers are getting short, the effective chairman can take the lead in lowering the profile of the issue to near-invisibility, in diminishing its significance to science, or in denying its real existence altogether—thus making it easy to move on to more tractable matters.
- The chairman will forestall the disruptive effects of the inevitable early departure of certain group members by stating, clearly and early, that any consensus or recommendations reached by the group at any point in the meeting will be binding on all participants, regardless of when they leave.
- Near the close of the session, the chairman will turn to the rapporteur for an informal summary of discussions and a listing of proposed conclusions and/or recommendations—and will then entertain comments and suggestions for changes.

- The meeting will end precisely at the time scheduled, and will never, never drag on into the evening hours, or even into the cocktail hour.
- The chairman will receive and review the rapporteur's report and distribute copies to all participants for comments. A final report will then be drafted and submitted to appropriate parties.

This listing of actions of chairmen of the varied scientific forums could grow to an intolerable length, but it won't do so here. The list gives a hint of the complexity and even the delicacy of the job, if it is done professionally—and to do it in such a manner is and should be a universal goal for any scientist, at any career stage, who finds himself so designated.

CHAPTER 8

SURVIVING THE CUT

"Cut Points" in Scientific Careers; The Special Traumas Associated with Grant Proposals; Fates of Those Who Do Not Survive the Cut; Personal Demons That Scientists Encounter

INTRODUCTION

One of the most thought-provoking short articles that I have read in a long time was published by John Tarkov in the *New York Times Magazine* (September 25, 1983). Titled "Making the Cut," its message (an obvious one) was that although the expression making or missing the cut—making the team or not making it—comes from the world of sports, the experience is universal. Although not specifically associated with science in the Tarkov article, the concept is as relevant there as it is in most human activities.

Surviving the cut is an indication of being good enough, when measured against peers or absolute performance standards, to move on to the next challenge.

Jim Sunderland's wife of three years still thinks he is great. True, she hasn't seen much of him in recent months, and when he is around he is impossible—totally preoccupied with his research and with where he is going in science. But as a postdoc in the second year of a two-year appointment in molecular biology, he has been somewhat understandably concerned about the future and where his career should be heading. King-size decisions have to be made quickly, such as: "Should it be another postdoc or a teaching position?" "What about joining a high tech company?" and "Is my area of research where I want to be?"

Of more immediate relevance, Jim, in exploring his options, has applied for, and has been interviewed for, an Assistant Professorship at a university 3000 miles away. The interview seemed to go well, with only a few rough spots (one faculty member asked him about his background in parasitology—which is remarkably close to nil—and a female assistant professor asked him about his attitudes toward women in science—a subject to which he had previously given very little thought). It was time now for the important letter of acceptance or rejection from that university.

Jim is fast approaching one of the many jagged edges of the "cut" system in science, in which he makes the cut *and is offered the job or* misses the cut *and becomes for the moment an also-ran.*

Some of the cuts in science are determined objectively but many decisions may be based on personal feelings as well; it is important to assess the relative weights of each component in preparing for the event. Some of the more obvious "cut points" in a professional career include (but are certainly not restricted to):

- Selection for a graduate student slot at a university of your choice (few things are more important in shaping a future career in science).
- Selection for a good, or even prestigious, graduate fellowship (preferably with a generous ''stipend'' attached).
- Selection for a postdoctoral fellowship (if this is the route you choose to follow) with an exceptional research group or with an outstanding individual scientist in your specific area of interest.
- Selection for an introductory-level teaching position at a major university or a college noted for academic excellence (again, at an adequate salary).
- Award of a first research grant, especially if it is in a highly competitive area (but *any* first grant is important).
- Award of a second and a third grant, especially if they are larger than the first and are based on insights and productivity demonstrated during the first grant period.
- Appointment to a review committee of a major and prestigious funding agency, particularly if it is a standing committee reporting to the agency head (but participation in *any* review committee at any level can be an instructive and rewarding as well as a time-consuming experience in which you learn how to conduct yourself in such an environment).

Decisions about the winners at many of the cut points already mentioned are made by science administrators (often, but not always, with advice from review groups). Other kinds of decisions are made by peers and colleagues, and they can affect scientific careers just as profoundly. Included are:

- Election to an office or to the board of directors of a scientific society representing your specialty.
- Selection as session chairman or symposium speaker at a national or international meeting.
- An invitation to membership on the organizing committee for a significant workshop, conference, or symposium in your specialty area.
- Designation as winner of an award for research accomplishment or excellence in teaching, in a process that requires selection by a committee of colleagues.
- A request to present a series of invited lectures, as part of an established annual event, in your specialty area.

"Making the cut" has relevance as well to research programs and results. The outpouring of technical information seems to increase in volume annually. Some of the information is significant and important to progress in a specialty area; much of it is useful but pedestrian; some of it is almost trivial. That part of research findings judged as the best by colleagues, reviewers, and journal editors survives the cut and becomes part of the foundation for future advances. That part judged less worthy by the same examiners may be published and then ignored, or it may be consigned to a file cabinet and disappear forever.

Some of the most severe and traumatic cuts in science involve decisions by granting agencies about funding proposed research. Early grants to beginning investigators are extraordinarily critical to career development, and rejections can be devastating—particularly for those pink-cheeked and unscarred ones who have not been through the rejection mill too often. Some perspective and a little peace of mind might be gained by considering the following:

- Junior professionals should realize that grant denials are almost as common in science as are manuscript rejections in writing novels.
- Junior professionals should realize that such denials can occur at any stage in a career; even senior people with good records of productivity can be turned down.
- Journeyman faculty people whose grant applications are rejected can be demoralized, since decisions about promotion and tenure may be influenced strongly by success or failure in grantsmanship.
- Some universities make a practice of paying faculty as part-time help, expecting them to make up the remainder of their salaries through grants. In such institutions, absence of grants can mean financial hardship for the unlucky faculty member.
- Some universities also make a practice of expecting basic equipment purchases to be made from grant funds, and not from institutional funds—even such basics as microscopes, analytical equipment, minicomputers, and office and laboratory furniture.
- Some universities charge maximum overhead on all grants and expect that a significant part of their operating funds will come from this source. Faculty members who do not get grants may be

seen as failing to make their expected contribution to the well-being of the organization.

Some scientists at one large Southeastern university have become so despondent and desperate about grants that they have signed up for a new administration-inspired self-help program to fund their own research. It is called the "Rent-A-Scientist Program" (RASP), in which a genuine degree-holding scientist makes himself available, at a price, for an evening cocktail party or a weekend in the country as "scientist in residence." The program has a dual purpose: (1) to help the scientist over an extended grant drought period and (2) to provide "acculturation"—acquainting the scientist with some of the folkways of upper yuppie America (many scientists are moderately asocial because of long years spent in laboratories; many have never played tennis or attended a country club dance; a few, almost unbelievably, have never found time to dally romatically or otherwise).

Graduated fees are charged, depending on the time to be invested by the scientist and the extent of his involvement. Some simple categories include:

- *Idle chatter over dinner (cheapest package).*
- *Informal guided field trip with commentary on scientist's specialty (such as wood-eating ants and cockroaches; worm parasites of fish).*
- *Evening slide show on a scientific topic (pseudo-seminar).*
- *Evening slide show accompanied by a microscope to amuse the kids.*
- *Evening slide show accompanied by a microscope and personal computer (with or without gee whiz lesson on computer use).*

- *More advanced evening seminar for families with precocious kids who already have a PC.*

The program organizers have found it necessary to develop some rules for the RASP sessions. These rules include:

- *Never hire more than one scientist for a party (they tend to cluster, to talk shop, and to argue among themselves— thereby not amusing the guests).*
- *Do not ask RASP scientists on assignment to baby-sit or to prepare dinner.*

The program has been very successful locally, and the organizers are now offering a franchise package for faculties of other colleges and universities.

Another approach to funding research projects has been limping along on the back roads of science for decades, but is now beginning to enter the main traffic routes, helped by the present Federal administration's massive unconcern about funding for nondefense projects. The core of the program is funding research by soliciting many tiny contributions from average people—*even graduate students. Solicitation can be enhanced if donors of small grants ($10 or more) are made to feel like an integral part of the research, through such devices as invitations to a kickoff cocktail party in the lab where the research is to be done, or having glassware to be used in the study etched with the donor's name, or selling T-shirts and sweatshirts custom-lettered with the research project title. Biologists have the greatest range of possibilities; for instance, they can promote an "Adopt-A-Porpoise" (or other experimental animal, from flatworm to whale) program, in which the cost of upkeep of the entire colony of experimental animals is prorated among the donors—who will be cited in the acknowledgments section of the technical paper that results from the study in which the animals are used.*

Additionally, donors will be guaranteed an author-autographed copy of the resulting paper (inscribed with a personal message for those who contribute more than the minimum). The investigator can incorporate as a nonprofit organization with tax-exempt status so donations will be tax-deductible, or the investigator can rent a post office box and form a foundation with an elaborate title, with a slick-paper brochure, and with members of his/her family consituting a board of directors.

The possible extensions of this "adoption" concept are almost limitless, depending on the ingenuity and imagination of the investigator and the amount of research time he is willing to devote to fund-raising. It can also be applied, for example, to field research. One interesting program was publicized recently in which finback whales, noted for distinguishing features visible to whale-watchers, could be "adopted" by donors to the research project. Contributors received a photo suitable for framing, a life history of "their" animal, and other inducements (one being a free whale-watching trip for a more-than-minimum donation). Any such proposed program should be well publicized, preferably with wide dissemination of a full-color brochure and with radio and television talk-show spots for the investigator and his staff of graduate students.

Still another approach to acquisition of research funding is a "Dial-A-Professor" *program, already being test-marketed in the southeastern United States. The program sets up a "hotline" to professors from students (including graduate students). Open-line telephones are used for questions about homework, reading assignments, exams, public issues, sex, or any topic within the professor's expertise. The participating professors could be paid at a fixed hourly rate (comparable to that of a neurosurgeon or a sex therapist) to be reimbursed by the univer-*

*sity or by charges to the caller's telephone bill (and sent to the
students' parents). The possible ramifications of this concept
are exciting. A panel of professors could be assembled live on
radio or television to respond to callers' queries; questions might
lead to subsequent counseling sessions and to a whole new vocation in public relations for those professors who prove adept
and amusing in such conversations. Best of all, students would
feel free (at a price) to indulge in games of "stump-the-
professor" as long as their money held out.*

*All these nickel-and-dime approaches to funding, while
they have some faint intrinsic value, should not obscure or
trivialize a very real current problem for academic scientists—
the drastic dwindling of financial support for research and the
severe impact the absence of grants can have on professional
careers.*

"Surviving the cut" in applying for grants is unques-
tionably important to the professional careers of academic scientists and requires some sensitivity to the
delicate mechanisms that separate acceptance from rejection. Full understanding of the decision-making
processes of funding agencies and organizations is beyond the mental capacities of most ordinary scientists.
Books have been written about ways to increase the
likelihood of success as an applicant; a few of the more
important guidelines have been culled out and assembled here:

- Each application must be a thing of beauty and
  substance—exuding knowledge of subject matter,
  with indications of precise knowledge of the proposed area of research and obvious enthusiasm for

the work ahead. As much time should be spent in preparing the application as would be spent later in writing up the results of the proposed work.

- The likelihood of success is improved significantly if some preliminary research in the area of the proposal has been done and some early indication of the potential value of the work has been achieved. Preliminary research should not be overemphasized in the proposal, however, because there is a danger that the funding agency could conclude that the work will be done anyway, whether funding is approved or not.

- The likelihood of success can also be increased by the presence in the proposal of names of co-investigators or consultants who have published extensively in the research area being proposed— and whose association with the project will be real. This need not imply, however, a major time commitment by such authorities.

- Study proposals that were *not* funded, to see whether flaws can be detected or other reasons for nonselection can be deduced.

- Unless specific instructions for proposal preparation are provided, submit more information than expected, but make sure it is well indexed and superbly prepared.

- Read books on grantsmanship; especially recommended is *The Individual's Guide to Grants* by J. B. Margolin (Plenum Press, 1983).

- The proposal must follow formal guidelines provided by the funding organization; more important, the proposed research must be in accord with the interests of that organization—interests that may shift in emphasis from year to year.

There follows an outline for the perfect grant proposal (in the absence of specific guidelines that would require another format):

INGREDIENTS OF THE PERFECT GRANT PROPOSAL

- *Executive summary*
- *Detailed description of the research plan:*
  - *Introduction*
  - *Application of expected research results*
  - *Preliminary experiments*
  - *Preliminary findings*
  - *Research objectives*
  - *Description of the research plan*
  - *Bibliography*
  - *Names and research experience of investigators (with résumés as appendixes)*
- *Timetable for completion*
- *Results expected*
- *Product expected (if applicable)*
- *Difficulties and risk mitigation*
- *Commercialization possibilities (if applicable)*
- *Economic value of the project*
- *Potential for other Federal and private funding*
- *Marketing strategy (if applicable)*
- *Relationships with other institutions*
- *Administration of the project—institutional and scientific*
- *Budget*
- *Budget justification*
- *Plan for evaluation—internal and external*

- *Appendixes—résumés (using standard single-page format); letters of support*

- The perfect grant proposal will be prepared meticulously on a word processor with capability for "print quality" reproduction; it will have a slick cover with color and a logo.
- Federal line agencies such as the Environmental Protection Agency, the Army Corps of Engineers, and the National Oceanic and Atmospheric Administration still have funds for extramural research, although the total nondefense pot seems to be diminishing. With such mission-oriented agencies, investigators should consider research *contracts* as well as research grants. These contracts are precisely defined and often require some shift in research emphasis by the investigator. Often, too, they require a multidisciplinary team to complete the required research. A critical component here is personal contact with good (if sometimes frustrated) government scientist-bureaucrats.
- Careful study should be made of the grant-proposal habits of faculty members with a good track record in funding—especially those who are away at national and international meetings, review panel sessions, and society committee meetings for much of the year, but whose grant-supported research seems to go on anyway.

Making or missing the cut, whether related to grants or any other rewards, can be a valuable operational concept throughout a scientific career, with particular relevance during the early uncertain years when decisions about relative worth are particularly critical.

Those who make the cut—who get the grants, the prizes, the tenure track positions, the promotions—have deservedly received much of the attention in this chapter. But what of all those who miss the cut, who are not selected as being good enough? What traumas do they endure; more important, what advice can be offered to them to prevent a recurrence?

Reactions to missing the cut are reflections of the individual's normal responses to other life situations:

- Some are completely destroyed and give up.
- Some withdraw to less competitive pursuits, often with lingering bitterness.
- Some persist, with no new goals or energy—just "treading water."
- Some reappear in new roles or create new niches for themselves.

The genuine professionals continue the struggle, rising up from the ashes, learning from past mistakes, and accepting defeats gracefully as part of the system of science, but not as eternal condemnation to exterior darkness. Most survivors will admit, though, that not surviving the cut can be emotionally disturbing, especially since many scientists have strong tendencies toward perfectionism, and the specter of being substandard in *anything* is not easy to cope with. There are, however, strategies available to those who fail but who refuse to be beaten by "the system." Discussions with survivors have led to a number of good points to be transmitted to others who may also miss the cut:

- Decisions against a candidate in any selection process do not indicate total worthlessness—just that some other person had qualifications that more precisely matched what was wanted.
- Decisions against a candidate may have hinged on minor factors or on personal biases of the person(s) making the decision.
- Often the reasons for nonselection are not made known to unsuccessful candidates, so that they are left to wonder for years or forever. Sometimes there is no objective answer, if the decision has been a subjective one—and sometimes *no* answer is more ego-preserving than an answer.
- After an initial period of shock, disbelief, and depression, the candidate who has been rejected should make an analysis of the entire sequence of events preceding the decision, attempting to focus on areas of weakness and strength.
- Whatever the nature of the cut—whether for a position, a promotion, a grant, or tenure—an early postrejection activity must be initial planning for an alternative strategy. Without some dynamic response, lethargy and unproductive daydreaming may assume control.
- Missing the cut in job selection may seem to be a critical blow to early career development, but it can be even more devastating if it occurs later in a career. As an example, if a scientist-administrator fails to be selected for a higher-level position, his *existing* position may become untenable, depending on the attitudes of the person selected. This is quite different from the situation with journeyman-

level positions, in which those not selected can continue in their existing jobs as integral parts of the organization. As another example, a decision about tenure can be extremely crucial to a mid-career professional, since in many institutions a negative decision is tantamount to dismissal, being followed often by a terminal contract.

- Missing the cut more than once should trigger serious attempts at self-analysis, to determine whether there may be some systematic deficiency, either personal or professional, that is impeding progress. This is not easy to do, and colleagues are not likely to volunteer much advice either. Spouses or good friends may be a little more open, but may not always have the right perspective on the problem.

The message of the cut, as described by Tarkov in the article mentioned at the beginning of this chapter, is: ''You are good enough'' or ''You aren't good enough''—joy or gloom—with no intergradation. But there is another and gentler message, too: ''Even if you miss the cut, have the grace and internal resources to continue.''

PERSONAL DEMONS THAT SCIENTISTS ENCOUNTER

This discussion of survival factors for new scientists would not seem complete without at least brief consideration of the down-side—the personal demons with which they must contend. Scientists as a group are remarkably private people, not especially noted for their willingness to share innermost feelings with others—even their closest colleagues. This makes any probe into personal lives a high-risk operation. Fortunately, during the long, difficult years of research conducted to provide background for this book, rare moments of unusual candor have occurred during interviews or during the waning moments of small-group cocktail parties in meeting hotels from Warsaw west to Honolulu. Scientists, like all people, have many fears and worries; some are based on realities and some are not. A few of these fears and worries are common among scientists but rare among the general population; these are of principal concern here.

In the list of concerns, worries, fears, and horrors— the personal demons that good scientists live with from day to day and often for their entire careers—a few stand out:

- One certainly has to be the *persistent fear of mediocrity*—of being just another faceless, white-coated figure in an anonymous laboratory somewhere, whose contributions do not excite the interest of the larger community and whose colleagues don't seem overly enthusiastic either.
- A close corollary to the aforementioned fear, particularly common among scientists of ''a certain age,'' is what has been described as the *fear of disappearance with insignificance*—of completing a scientific career without ever having made even a modestly important contribution to the evolution of a hypothesis or the emergence of a concept.

- Another very real fear, prevalent among those working in rapidly developing high technology areas, is that of *falling back from a leadership position* in the race to attain specific research objectives— which are often the same objectives of other research teams. There is room for just so many winners; the others become also-rans.
- Related to this fear is the *fear of losing priority of discovery* because some other individual or group has published results days or weeks in advance of the publication date of your major paper—or, even worse, a competitor has released news of a discovery to the media before you could do the same.
- Still another real fear is that of *misinterpretation of data—of being wrong*, especially if such an error is brought to attention after a paper has been published. This fear is enhanced in today's climate of rapid publication and inadequate time for quiet contemplation of data.

Underlying these major fears is a whole writhing snake pit of worries that can beset scientists; some are daily companions, some assume larger proportions on specific occasions. They include:

- Worry about being involved, against one's better judgment, in *public controversies* about scientific matters—especially in issues with high emotional content, such as accusations of fraud.
- Concern about *continuing ability to attract strong grant support* (or even any grant support at all) in a chosen research area.

- Worry about the *long-term stability of the employing institution*, in view of the restricted student populations and persistent funding droughts.
- Worry about *what constitutes a satisfactory rate of personal progress*, in terms of rank, salary, perks, and recognition—and about whether ''satisfactory'' is enough as a career objective.
- Worry about that ultimate stamp of failure— *dismissal or negative tenure decision*.

Added to the long list of concerns, worries, and fears that are part of everyday life—about disabling illness, accidents, alcoholism, divorce, and nuclear war—these additional job-related burdens can at times become mildly overwhelming. To the consummate dedicated worrier, these superimposed professional burdens can be seized upon and exploited with great delight. Fortunately, they are often counterbalanced by successes in science—or by tangible evidence that at least some (and often many) of the fears are groundless and safely confined to our nightmares.

A final element in this enumeration of demons is one that is almost universal—the *difficulty in maintaining and managing a satisfactory personal life while still pursuing career objectives*. The problem is especially acute for new scientists, who are under the greatest pressures to produce, to publish, and to excel. Some become obsessed with succeeding professionally, to the point where all other aspects of living become insignificant and blurred. Some are not even aware of the obsession or, if they are, rationalize it as a necessary but temporary imbalance. The reality is that behavior patterns like these can become fixed, and their persistence can result in a sterile, unidimensional existence, devoid of most human contacts and productive only of scientific data. This is too narrow a focus for any life.

Good scientists make deliberate choices that can provide a better balance between personal lives and careers. Some common techniques include self-imposed dicta about "never bringing laboratory problems home in the evening," "never spending weekends in the laboratory or writing technical papers," or "always planning vacations that are absolutely unrelated to science" (and not tacked onto a scientific meeting). It is hard to follow such dicta, though. Science is for many such an all-absorbing profession that it is easy to slip back into evil ways that suppress or eliminate most of the joys of close association with family and friends. The struggle must be a never-ending one, but it is one that is often lost.

But enough of this talk of demons and failures! Scientists as a group tend to cope with distractions and stresses as well as people in any occupation, and often they do better at it than some other professionals (physicians and lawyers, for example). Coping is an adaptive response; its elements are best ingrained early in any career.

CHAPTER 9

RECRUITMENT AND RECRUITING

Guidelines for Potential Recruits; Balance Sheets for Entry-Level Positions; Recruiter's Dilemmas

INTRODUCTION

Some of the most critical people interactions in science are those clustered around the process of filling vacant or new positions. Whether in research, teaching, research and teaching, or management, there are two distinct perspectives—that of the person being recruited and that of the person(s) doing the recruiting. Innumerable guidelines could be proposed for those on each side of the fence, but especially for those being recruited. Since this book is oriented toward the entry-level professional, most of this chapter focuses, sensibly, on those being recruited.

The contact period that will help determine success in acquiring the job may be distressingly short, consisting of an interview with a Department Chairman or Dean or both, or it may be very long, consisting of a seminar followed by several almost endless days of intensive grilling by present faculty or staff members, singly or in small groups. This contact time, and the impressions made, may be truly critical to selection, or it may be a facade, if a preselection for the job has already been made by the Dean or Department Chairman. There is often no easy way to determine which game is being played, so the only option available to the applicant is to assume that the wheel has not been rigged in advance.

The preparatory steps to be taken before facing the very important cut period of selection or rejection for a job in science can be grouped into three categories: (1) long-term, (2) near-term, and (3) short-term. Most of the really critical preparation has to be *long-term*—a solid foundation in science, excellent ability to present thoughts orally, self-confidence without overconfidence, a physical appearance commensurate with the hoped-for position—selection factors that you can't buy or cram for.

Beyond these, *near-term* steps should be considered seriously during the several months immediately preceding departure from the protective ecosystem of the university graduate department or the safe, if temporary, cocoon of a postdoctoral fellowship. Some of the near-term measures are easy, others are less so, but all can enhance visibility and desirability in the job market. A few that seem feasible are:

- Publish early and well—preferably in major journals and preferably with your thesis advisor. Precocious paper production can be an important factor in decisions about first interviews and first jobs.

- Write an outstanding letter of application, presenting yourself as a professional able to augment significantly the present staff and research efforts of the institution. Such a letter should be accompanied by appropriate documents, especially publications.

- Write and send the perfect résumé, one that emphasizes current professional information rather than past events and that is prepared on a high-quality word processor.

- Give very careful thought to letters of recommendation. Insofar as possible, people who write those letters must know you as a person as well as a scientist, and it is helpful if they are known to at least one member of the institutional search committee. In asking for such letters, it is better to be frank but delicate—indicating that if the person cannot write a positive letter, you would prefer to know it and to select someone else.

- If the prospective job is with a government agency, many additional rules and strictures apply. Any interaction with government bureaucrats is difficult, beyond the form-letter level. It is important to write an initial letter to a *person* and not just to an *office*. Be prepared to be ignored and then to send a follow-up letter, followed in turn by a phone call to the *appropriate contact level*—too high, and you irritate; too low, and you get no response from the system. The key in such initial contacts is to be aggressive but very polite, emphasizing your particular talents or expertise. If available, internships or temporary positions are advantageous, since they allow you to study this complex system from within and place you in a favorable position for something a little more permanent. Additionally, contacts with the agency through state and Federal legislators can be productive at an entry level. Persistence is an absolute requisite, though, especially in the current climate of funding reductions in some programs and concomitant restrictions on hiring new government employees.

Beyond the near-term job-hunting steps just listed, some *short-term* preparatory steps can be taken (assuming that you have survived initial screening and have been invited to the institution for an obligatory and highly stressful interview). They include such obvious measures as these:

- Review the literature in your area of presumed expertise, so that you can discuss it comfortably and adequately if pressured by an inquisitor.
- Project *enthusiasm* for your own research and for science in general.
- Develop (and even write down) potential questions that could be asked by inquisitors during the job interview—and then outline well-rounded responses to them.
- Review in your own mind your existing contributions to science, being sure that you have a well-thought-out plan for your future research

activities—which should be in accord with your perception of what the institution expects.

- Prepare, if the job involves teaching, to project knowledge of good teaching methods and approaches—preferably from your own experience.
- Review your attitudes toward personal relationships in science, ethics in science, and women in science.
- Reexamine your record in grant applications and research funding, and give some consideration to your future grant proposal plans, so that you can discuss these matters easily.
- Provide a number of copies of your résumé to the laboratory/department head, so that most of the inquisitors will have had the opportunity to review your qualifications at their leisure if they wish (some won't bother, of course, until five minutes before the session).

In addition to these obvious short-term measures, there are other steps that could be taken but are not so obvious:

- Get an up-to-date list of current professional staff/faculty members (if only from the catalog) and find out the specialties of key members who may well turn up as inquisitors. Then try to indicate during the interview that you are aware of their great contributions to science (but only if you take the time to make yourself aware).
- Spend some time with the book *American Men and Women of Science* (15th ed., Cattell Press, eds., R. R. Bowker, New York, 1982), so that you will have

some knowledge of the ages, specialties, and interests of the staff/faculty people who may form part of the interview team (this is particularly important for the Dean and Department Chairman).

- If a seminar or a series of seminars is to be part of the selection process, invest at least three times the number of hours that you might otherwise spend in preparation, being absolutely positive that timing, visuals, and presentation of results are not just good, but impeccable, and that the presentation has breadth beyond your own work.

- Recognize that physical appearance is, to some inquisitors at least, an important factor. Simple things like appropriate clothes and clean fingernails should not be discounted.

- Keep in mind the easily overlooked point that such inquisitions may be stressful to members of the interview group as well as to you—in that they are expected to ask intelligent, relevant questions that will lead to proper evaluation of candidates, without revealing inadequacies in their own retentive abilities or breadth of knowledge.

- Avoid overt signs of excessive nervousness during the interview—which can make the whole process a less-than-pleasant event for everybody.

- The recruitment interview is a time when what you are, in terms of ability, intellect, background, attitudes, and accomplishments, will be on the line as at few other times in an entire career. At other times, you can plead ignorance, bluster, obfuscate, withdraw, or deny—but not at this interview.

I recently witnessed an excellent illustration of the value of preparation for the all-important final selection process. A large New England university was recruiting for an entry-level position, and the list of candidates had been cut to three. Each was invited to appear on the campus in turn, to present a seminar and to ''chat'' with current faculty members (the chats turned out to be a succession of half-hour inquisitions by small groups of staff members).

Candidate A *did well in presenting the seminar, but concentrated totally on somewhat pedestrian and narrowly oriented research. The interviews later also disclosed a restricted view of the discipline and a vagueness about future plans for research. Responses to questions were guarded and surrounded by caveats.*

Candidate B *gave a good seminar presentation, couching personal research in the broader context of knowledge in the discipline area. She was direct and enthusiastic during the interviews and seemed to actually enjoy the give and take with faculty members.*

Candidate C *also gave a reasonable seminar presentation, with adequate responses during the discussion. The subsequent interviews were painful, though, since he reacted defensively to questions and was clearly ill at ease during the sessions— to the extent that some responses were mumbled and almost inaudible.*

Later discussions with the department chairman and written comments from members of the various interview teams disclosed that although all three candidates appeared in their résumés to be qualified scientifically for the position, the on-site performances weighed heavily in favor of Candidate B, and she was subsequently picked for the job. I wondered at the time—and I still wonder—whether the unsuccessful candidates ever understood the reasons why they were not selected.

All the foregoing suggestions and admonitions might be useful, but there are no guarantees. The selection process is ultimately a subjective one, and what seem to be strong points in your favor may actually be perceived as deficiencies. Good research may be viewed as too narrow or too ''practical,'' self-confidence may be interpreted as ''cockiness,'' and interest in good teaching may be seen as disinterest in research. The situation isn't ''no-win,'' however, since excellent credentials are not easy to ignore.

BALANCE SHEETS FOR ENTRY-LEVEL POSITIONS

Often, while selection committees and administrators are interviewing applicants for science positions, it becomes apparent that these prospective employees are pretty naïve—that they have made only a superficial analysis of the benefits and pitfalls of each of the principal types of science employment (university, industry, and government). This is a dreadful state of affairs, considering that a decision about type of employment is one of the most important to be made in an entire career. The acquisition of *any* position in science is difficult, but there is no excuse for inadequate assessment of advantages and disadvantages—even for temporary jobs. Many personal preferences enter into selection of the type of employment in science, but each major employer group—university, industry, and government—has particular favorable and unpleasant attributes. Some of these are listed in Table 1, one section of which summarizes benefits and the other pitfalls.

From an examination of this table, it is obvious that nobody promises a rose garden. Perspectives on type of employment depend to a great degree on individual attitudes, as well as on availability of niches. Some new scientists thrive in an environment in which other new scientists are totally miserable. For example, some prosper in team-oriented, hard-driving, industrial development laboratories, whereas others much prefer the academic calm and independent research of a midsize university department. Whatever the workplace characteristics, it behooves any recruit to match them with his/her own personal preferences before signing an employment agreement.

RECRUITING

At a recent scientific society meeting in Canada, I heard an assistant professor serving on an evening panel state that "old-boy networks" no longer apply in today's job market. Reaction from the audience was instantaneous and audible, and later comments suggested widespread disagreement with his point of view. A few participants even offered first-hand evidence to disprove it. During the cocktail party that followed the panel session, I asked some of the attendees what they thought of this interesting exchange. Many of the participants were not at all sure what an "old-boy network" was, but concluded that it had to be something repugnant. Others

TABLE 1. BENEFITS AND RISKS OF SCIENTIFIC EMPLOYMENT

University	Industry	Government
Employment benefits		
A familiar academic environment with opportunity to explore new research areas. Challenges and satisfactions in organizing and presenting courses in specialty area. Satisfactions in meaningful contacts with interested and well-prepared students, at graduate and undergraduate levels. Pleasures in informal daily contacts with upwardly mobile, well-trained peers and more senior colleagues.	Salary in a range that permits repayment of earlier loans and a standard of living compatible with professional expectations. Equipment usually state of the art and with adequate technician support. Encouragement for postdoctoral training and opportunity for professional travel. Colleagues often among ''the best and the brightest.''	Reasonably stable research environment despite vagaries in funding. Equipment budgets usually adequate, even though acquisition may be on ''feast-or-famine'' schedule. Programs usually well defined, with remarkable continuity despite popular misconceptions. Salary and fringe benefits excellent, despite recent nibbling by political administrations. Promotion potential excellent for demonstrated producers.
Employment pitfalls		
Entrenched tenured senior faculty, some of whom no longer have a real interest in science. Hierarchy of business-oriented administrators. Low starting salary and minuscule annual raises, leading	Company may be paranoid about release of data through publication. Restrictive employment contracts prevent normal dialogue with colleagues. Company may revise its corporate struc-	Changes in administration invariably reverberate down through the career bureaucracy, affecting research groups as well as service groups. Some agencies are narrowly mission-oriented, and judg-

TABLE 1. *(Continued)*

University	Industry	Government
Employment benefits		
to a perpetual scramble for an adequate standard of living.	ture, with the new organization unable or unwilling to support preexisting research effort.	ments of scientific worth of products may be colored by that orientation.
Constant stress from required grant acquisition as source of funding for the institution and for graduate student support.	Research supervisors and managers may be totally business-oriented, without sensitivity for value of research.	Agency directors and their appointees are often not scientists, and they may de-emphasize research functions by withdrawing funds.
Often heavy teaching loads with many lab sections and endless student conferences in undergraduate courses.	Junior people may be hired with elaborate titles, but their actual duties may be subprofessional or even clerical.	Tenure in government positions is almost immutable—for the incompetent as well as the competent.
Necessity to grind out publications constantly, as evidence of ''scholarly achievement'' (the classic ''publish or perish'' syndrome, which is still very much alive in most university science departments).	Junior people may be hired in superabundance, but may be winnowed out severely in the first year, only a few being retained.	Initial civil service positions are hard to get, the best route being through very uncertain ''temporary'' jobs.
Difficulty in discerning real institutional attitudes on teaching vs. research and in achieving a personally satisfactory balance of these professional responsibilities.	Interminable strictures and quibbles over patents.	

thought it meant a system in which members of ''the club'' used their influence to ensure selection of the other club members' Ph.D. candidates for available positions. Still others thought it meant that informal networks, operating among club members, transmitted the word about good positions that were open or would be open, well in advance of any public announcement. A generally accepted definition of an ''old-boy network'' probably does not exist, but its essence would be ''a system of communication and mutually supportive activities perpetuated by established members of a subdiscipline.'' Whatever the definition, the implication was clear—that methods of announcing vacancies and selecting candidates beyond those accepted as standard Equal Employment Opportunity practices are in operation. This may be true for many science positions, especially those in universities.

Selection techniques may vary from institution to institution, but the appearance of a newly recruited faculty member or staff member elicits a mixed bag of responses from existing faculty or staff, again based on individual perceptions:

- *Relief*—if the position has been vacant for a year or more and present faculty has had to fill in.
- *Disbelief*—that anyone as young as the recruit could have a Ph.D., let alone postdoctoral experience and several publications (some of the new people do look like undergraduates).
- *Curiosity*—especially about the recruit's starting salary compared to the present salaries of long-time faculty members.

- *A vague sense of unease*—about professional back-grounds acquired so long ago, when compared with the obvious state-of-the-art status of the recruit's information.
- *Uncertainty*—about why the university did not recruit at a more senior level for a new faculty member with established reputation and status in a specialty.
- *Concern*—that this action represents part of a program to phase out long-time faculty as quickly as possible and to replace them with relatively inexpensive newcomers.
- *Pleasure*—that the institution has been able to attract and hire an obviously well-qualified new scientist (or, conversely, amazement at the absence of superior qualifications among the applicants from which the recruit was chosen).

Recruiting, then, regardless of the problems that the process presents to administrators, is a bittersweet experience for existing faculty and staff, combining the pleasure of participating in selecting competent if very junior colleagues and the worry about disturbing a comfortable status quo in the department.

CHAPTER 10

CHARACTERISTICS OF SCIENCE WORKPLACES

A Proposed Method for Quantitative Evaluation of Research Environments; Locating the Individual in Science Hierarchies; Science Libraries; A Role for Intellectual Snobs; "Authority Figures" in Science

INTRODUCTION

The *kinds* of science workplaces would seem at first glance almost to defy categorization. A little casual reflection, though, discloses some methods of grouping that can be useful for descriptive purposes at least. One mode of subdivision is obvious—that based on the *type of organization*: academic (university), government, industrial, or private foundation. Once that initial vertical grouping is made, it is then possible to prepare a lateral perspective based on *nature of leadership*, ranging from autocratic/dictatorial to completely permissive. Then the whole thing can be expanded (as I've done in Figure 6) into a three-dimensional matrix by adding such categories as *nature of funding sources* (e.g., grants, institutional funds, public funds, private bequests), the *extent of support staff and services* (ranging from none and miserable to adequate and excellent), the *availability of in-service training or sabbaticals or both* (ranging from nonexistent to great), the *encouragement of interactions beyond the organization* (e.g., multiinstitutional grants, travel to national and international meetings, seminars, and symposia presented at other institutions), and the *table of organization* (e.g., degree of formality of structure, relationships among occupants of various hierarchical steps, kinds of comunication channels).

Once all the appropriate boxes of the matrix have been inked in, *a vague three-dimensional composite of any research organization will begin to emerge*—one that can be augmented by second-order or satellite matrices (see Figure 6) built around assessments of faculty relationships, student attitudes, degree of freedom to act as consultants, and others, if the organization is a teaching as well as a research entity. Other second-order matrices can be based on peer–colleague interactions alone, including assessment of effective communications—formal and informal—within the group, the frequency of seminars and discussion groups, and even the extent of intrainstitutional socializing among group members. Still other second-order matrices could be built on assessments of the vitality of the organization, as demonstrated by the extent of ongoing research, volume of publications, and current professional recognition of staff members.

Analysis of all these completed primary and secondary matrices for any organization could lead to a reason-

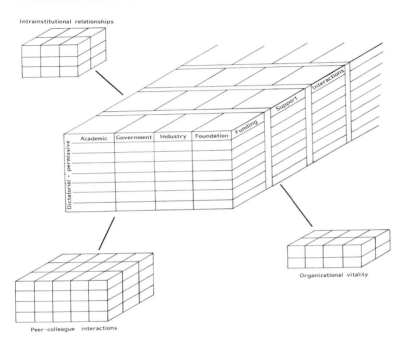

FIGURE 6. Model for evaluating science workplaces.

ably reliable evaluation of the kind of research environment to be expected there. *Such an evaluation should be a factor in any decision to join or not to join a particular group.*

Here, then, is probably the principal contribution of this chapter—*a proposed method for quantitative evaluation of research environments.* Beyond this, though, there are many other aspects of science workplaces that should be discussed. A few that I want to consider are:

- Survival and death in the hierarchies of science
- Science libraries and their use
- Intellectual superiority and intellectual snobbery within the organization
- The role of "authority figures" in scientific groups

SURVIVAL AND DEATH IN THE HIERARCHIES OF SCIENCE

The entire concept of "hierarchies" in science is repugnant to some purists who want to get on with the real business of science, which is to them the production and publication of new information, without involvement in "games" or "strategies" or "management." To most practitioners, however, the many scientific hierarchies are realities and are factors to be considered seriously as professional careers develop. Since this book is aimed at new scientists, some elementary education in the nature and complexities of these scientific hierarchies would seem to be a necessary exercise. A logical entry point (as usual) would be a listing of the principal hierarchies that will be encountered. They include:

- *Institutional hierarchies*—a succession of ranks within the organization, academic or other.
- *Professional society hierarchies*—from new members to the board of directors to the president.
- *"In-group" hierarchies*—from the acolytes to the gurus who make up the innermost governing circle.
- *Publication hierarchies*—from occasional reviewers to the long-term journal editor.
- *Research grant hierarchies*—from the recipient of a tentative and minuscule institutional faculty grant

to the director of a major multiinstitutional and multidisciplinary grant.

Many good ways of visualizing the dynamics and complexities of scientific hierarchies undoubtedly exist. One simplistic approach is the concept of an intersecting and interlocking framework of ladders, each of which can represent one of the five listed hierarchies. According to this visualization, the ladders form a kind of vertically interlocking Jungle Gym for adults; intersections may be at lower rungs for some factors and at higher rungs for others. For example, a good scientist may be on a high rung in competence, but if he eschews anything but minimal participation in professional societies, then he would be on a low rung of the "professional society hierarchy" ladder. As another example, a science administrator might be on a high rung of the "institutional hierarchy" ladder, but low in scientific credibility among colleagues, hence on a low rung of the "in-group hierarchy." If it makes any sense at all, this concept results in the formation of a complex, delicately balanced structure, the interlocking rungs of which may prove slippery if the climber makes a misstep (e.g., midlife crisis, accusations of fraud, intralaboratory sexual adventure). According to this dismal concept, the entire career of a scientist is spent scrambling up (and sometimes down) ladders or transferring temporarily from one ladder to another, in attempts to keep from falling off.

Viewed in another way, but still using remnants of the ladder concept, each scientific career can be represented by a *graph* representing a composite of positions in the numerous hierarchies of science, as presented in Figure 7. Each professional can then be described as a graph with a fixed shape at any moment

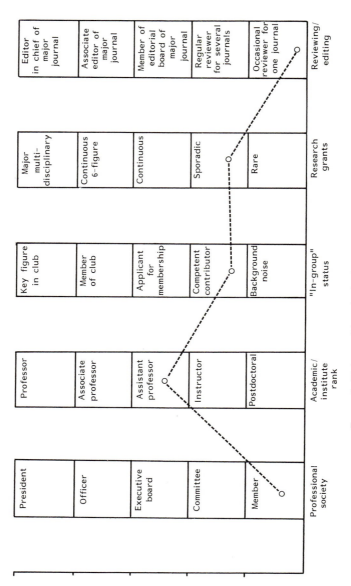

FIGURE 7. Major positions in the hierarchies of science.

in time during his/her career (an example is superimposed on the figure). Analysis of such a personal graph and how its shape evolves over time can provide insights into the nature and progress of that individual. This can lead to an entire complex science of graph analysis looking at specific decades of professional existence and leading to characterization of the individual scientist as "early achiever," "late bloomer," "organization-oriented," or "people-conscious," according to how the shape of his/her personal graph evolves. The graph can be used in self-analysis or as a basis for career counseling advice. (Maybe this system already exists. It seems elementary enough to have been elaborated long ago, but I have not encountered it in science, although a close counterpart is used in evaluation of industrial and government managers and supervisors and in their management training programs.)

The objective is not necessarily to push all points on the graphs to their highest levels, but rather to help scientists to *recognize* their strengths and weaknesses in hierarchical competition—if such competition is important to them (and to some it is not).

This concept of hierarchical analysis could make an interesting cocktail-party game—having one volunteer do a self-evaluation and then having colleagues prepare graphs anonymously, based on *their* perceptions of the person being evaluated. This must be carefully handled though, to ensure ego preservation.

Additionally, the concept might be used to quantify faculty committee discussions about promotion or tenure—since it supplies some modicum of objectivity, if the evolution of graphs is studied and interpreted in accord with standards that could be prepared and incorporated in a user's manual that could be written on the method (but not by me).

In thinking about this whole matter of scientific hierarchies, one comes rather quickly to the obvious conclusion that caveats, elaborations, and qualifications need to be made to the admittedly primitive presentation just outlined. Some that have occurred to me (and you will certainly have others) are:

- Other types of hierarchies should probably be included—such as those involved in training new scientists or in managing research groups.
- Interdependence exists among the hierarchies, but rates of ascent can be determined by individual preferences and degrees of commitment as well as by ability.
- Expectations and responsibilities increase at higher levels of each hierarchy (and the model does not deal with this).
- The number of niches (which might be represented by the size of the rungs or compartments) decreases as each hierarchy is ascended.
- *Descent* as well as ascent of some of the hierarchies is a reality during most professional careers; for example, society offices are remarkably and properly transient.

A combination of the two approaches outlined in this section—analysis of the nature of science workplaces and examination of the kinds of hierarchies that exist in science—should help to orient the new scientist trying to fit his own personal characteristics to a particular type of professional environment. This is a useful end in itself, but in addition there are special attributes of science workplaces—libraries, attitudes of colleagues, and "in-group" influences—that deserve additional comment. They will receive it in the following sections.

SCIENCE LIBRARIES AND THEIR USE

Good institutional science libraries are sources of joy and comfort to any professional; they are also a critical component of the science workplace. Too often, though, they are taken for granted and are considered part of the "givens" in any equation used in assessing the relative desirability of the institution as a place in which to do research and teaching. They deserve greater attention from scientists who are staff members, as well as from those who are about to become members. Discussions with science librarians during the preparation of this volume have been informative, and from them I have distilled (as is my custom) some suggestions and admonitions:

- Visit the department/laboratory/institute/university library often; librarians really love their constituents passionately, but often they don't see enough of them even for name recognition.
- Pick a half dozen journals and (1) *scan* them with great regularity, (2) *read summaries or abstracts* of all articles, and (3) *read entire articles* in your specialty area.
- So that you will have some acquaintance with happenings in the big world outside the laboratory or department, scan (weekly) *Science* and *Nature* and

(monthly) *Scientific American*—page by page, including the book reviews, letters to the editor, editorials, and positions available. Also include one or more publications in any foreign language(s) you are able to read.

- After reading an article relevant to your specialty and worth remembering or referencing some day, write for a reprint or, better still (in the great likelihood of nonresponse to reprint requests), make a copy of the article immediately for your expanding indexed reprint collection.

- Make a monthly pilgrimage to the new-book shelf to see who is leading in the ''editorship'' game and who has written a book that you should have written.

- If an article in your specialty seems particularly well written or innovative, or proposes a new aspect of research, write to the senior author (with copies to the other authors) and tell him/her of your pleasure and profit from reading the offering. The cost in time and postage is minute in proportion to the satisfactions to the author(s).

- If your library has a scientific committee to aid in the selection of books and journals, and to consider other scientific questions, volunteer for it. We all know that libraries are important supports for every scientific organization, so why not invest a little time on your own turf to improve that essential support activity?

- Abuses of library holdings—books and journals—are common in teaching institutions, especially by undergraduates, but (unfortunately) also by graduate students. The abuses include, but are definitely not limited to, tearing articles from bound journals, theft of bound journals, theft of books, and theft of current issues of journals. Such intolerable acts by those on the "lunatic fringe" of science result in the imposition of strict rules that may at times seem oppressive—library cards with photographs, alarm systems to prevent removal of nondeactivated coded holdings, turnstiles for checkout (yes, turnstiles), and closed stacks for journal holdings.

Without traffic, libraries are tidy but desolate places. Go there, for information, for quiet contemplation, or to ponder the meaning of all your accumulated knowledge.

INTELLECTUAL SUPERIORITY AND INTELLECTUAL SNOBBERY WITHIN THE ORGANIZATION

Multitudes of extremely bright, highly trained, and super-productive people can be found in scientific organizations—a not-too-profound statement considering the complexity of some of the problems to be solved. Such people *are* superior organisms and as such deserve respect and support. Geniuses, even among scientists, are not abundant; most of us have "high-normal" or "near-genius" IQ status and act like normal earthlings most of the time.

Occasionally, though, as in any occupation demanding mental exertion, it is possible to identify individuals who must be characterized as "intellectual snobs." While they may make brilliant contributions in their fields, they tend to be "low-normal" in people relationships, primarily because of their great disdain for average intellects. They usually have only superficial interest in the broader aspects of science and are impatient with discussions outside their narrow specialty area. They usually know their IQ scores to the second decimal place and luxuriate in that knowledge. They tend to converse in a code consisting mostly of jargon and usually confine their discussions to the few others in the same specialty whom they consider to be their intellectual near-peers.

Snobs of this ilk are difficult to cope with in the laboratory, the classroom, or elsewhere in the scientific enterprise. They are often abrasive and often determinedly deficient in rudimentary social skills. They do not "suffer fools gladly"—nor do they suffer even average intellects gladly.

But, we need them. They may perceive problems and solutions to problems sooner and better than most others; they may see with great clarity a course of action that is obscure to others; they may motivate colleagues to examine issues with broader perspectives. A primary catalytic role for geniuses may not atone for all their transgressions, but it lessens the trauma of daily association and occasionally produces small islands of brilliant light in an otherwise dimly illuminated landscape.

THE ROLE OF "AUTHORITY FIGURES" IN SCIENTIFIC GROUPS

One of the most influential but also the least precisely defined hierarchies in science is the "in group" or "club" in any narrow subdiscipline. Such groups are dominated by so-called "authority figures"—usually those who have made significant contributions to research and concept development in that subdiscipline. Members of the inner circle of in groups are often fiercely competitive and intolerant of "outsiders." Furthermore, members of the in group often develop restricted perspectives that lead to abuses:

- Members of the in group may impose on the specialty area a form of "dictatorship of the orthodox" (translated as *their* views) and indulge in carefully circumspect ridicule of those who have other views.
- Members of the in group maintain a reward–demerit system to judge those newcomers who would join the club.
- Members of the in group may use "state-of-the-art technology" (or its absence) to exclude non-members of the club from "serious professional consideration." This seems to be at the moment a particular forte of biochemists; club members exclude newcomers who have not learned their methodology at the knee of a club member.
- Members of the in group often serve as editors or editorial board members of "serious scientific journals" and can have some influence on what is published and even what is cited.
- Members of the in group serve on grant evaluation panels and can influence decisions of grant administrators about what areas should be explored, who should get the funds, and how much they should get.

Having said all these negative things about ''in groups'' and ''authority figures,'' I think it only fair to include some positive attributes as well:

- Authority figures in science occupy their positions because of demonstrated competence, innovation, and productivity in their specialties. There is no alternate route, although organizational abilities and interpersonal skills certainly help smooth the passage.
- Authority figures and their students can do much to initiate and expand research in an area previously neglected or not even envisioned.
- Authority figures and their students (and their students in turn) can ensure continuity and depth of inquiry into basic research problems.
- Authority figures act as gate-keepers in science, adept at recognizing the few charlatans who may appear in the guise of scientists.
- Authority figures may act as referees, serving on select committees formed to investigate and resolve controversies that develop among colleagues.
- Authority figures contribute to the ''self-policing'' that has otherwise become a disappearing characteristic of science.
- Authority figures serve as role models for new generations of scientists—demonstrating the importance of excellence and professionalism in science.

Scanning the favorable and unfavorable aspects of a system influenced so much by ''authority figures'' and ''in groups,'' one must conclude that they are significant bulwarks against anarchy and chaos in scientific research. They form a critical if somewhat nebulous part of the infrastructure, even though defects may exist.

This treatment of science workplaces has been obviously diffuse—ranging from evaluation of research environments to consideration of the role of "authority figures" and "in groups." A common objective, if one exists, is to prepare new scientists for occupancy of their chosen habitats, by emphasizing some of the characteristic features of those habitats—good and bad. So much more could be said and probably should be said, but not here, since the number of proposals and concepts has already reached burdensome levels. Suffice it to say in conclusion that the *environment* in which scientific research is conducted has many facets—most of which affect the inhabitants in some way, positively or otherwise. Knowledge of how these environments are structured is important to all, but to the new scientist in particular.

CHAPTER 11

TRANSACTIONS AND COMPROMISES IN SCIENCE

The Credit–Debit System among Scientists—Deposits and Withdrawals; The Daily Prostitutions of Compromises in Science; Scientists for Hire—Consulting Experiences for New Scientists

INTRODUCTION

Scientific games have been variously described in this book as "interpersonal strategies on the margins of science" or more elaborately as "transactions that legitimately enhance progress in the many person-to-person relationships that surround the act of doing good science." The *transactional* component of scientific games has been underemphasized in most discussions, even though it can be an important general operating principle. Many interpersonal activities surrounding science involve "transactions"—in which *points or credits are acquired from or given to colleagues.* This happens almost automatically in most instances. Credits are acquired by such actions as accepting seminar invitations from colleagues at other institutions, being willing to accept a colleague's graduating senior as a graduate student, finding a postdoctoral slot for a colleague's Ph.D. candidate, serving on a time-demanding society committee, filling in for several lectures in a colleague's class so he can do some field studies or attend a foreign symposium, supporting a colleague orally in evaluation committee meetings, actively supporting a supervisor's position during discussion of a critical organizational issue, generously including marginal contributors as authors of a scientific paper, and a host of similar acts. Conversely, credits are lost and debits incurred by the receiving of such favors.

The perceived donor–recipient relationship, while usually unstated, is real and is very much a part of the fabric of science. Ingredients of the relationship include:

- A necessary common perception by donor and recipient of the extent of the donation.
- Continual rough tally of points gained or lost by all participants, so that members of each donor–recipient pair can assess their balances at any time.
- Assessment by each professional of the total extent to which he/she can contribute to the credit bank, balancing this against other career responsibilities (e.g., personal research, writing, student contact).
- Assessment by each professional of the extent to which he/she can draw on credits with any other colleague without danger of resistance or rejection.

The credit–debit system works best among colleagues who are peers—approximately equal in status, age, and accomplishments—so that points can be traded at par. Colleagues who are out of phase with respect to any of these attributes encounter a weighted system of credits–debits. A junior colleague, for example, must expect that acquisition of points will be more difficult and that fewer points will be awarded for any given act. A more senior colleague, with a record of major accomplishments in a specialty, should expect more credits for any given act from colleagues who are not peers.

This credit–debit system is of course common among politicians, lawyers, used-car salesmen, army supply sergeants, antique dealers, and many other categories of people with special interests. Some observers even extrapolate the system to everyday life and to the numerous transactions that occur each day with all kinds of individuals. Our interest here is in the particular nuances of the system that affect practicing scientists, not in proclaiming the discovery of a concept unique to science. It is safe to conclude, however, that many professionals participate in the credit–debit system of science without adequate analysis of its career impact and without recognition of its ground rules (some would reject such rules anyway).

For those scientists willing to play with a concept, and to consider its implications in their careers, I propose a "Code of Practice" to govern transactions with colleagues, recognizing that countless exceptions and qualifications will exist:

- Place a realistic maximum value on your time, your stature in the field, and your contribution to any transaction.
- In making requests, do not underestimate a col-

league's perception of the worth of his time, stature, and contributions.

- Tread cautiously in any transactions involving ''authority figures'' in a specialty area; their self-perceptions may be inflated (legitimately or not).
- Assess any request from colleagues first in terms of impact on your personal research time and preexisting commitments; only then can other rules of the credit–debit system apply.
- Recognize that withdrawals from the credit bank must be balanced by deposits; temporary deficits may be tolerated by colleagues, but not for long.
- In agreeing to a request for any major commitment, make sure that the requester has a realistic appraisal (yours) of the extent of that commitment.
- Occasionally, accept with enthusiasm a request from a junior colleague to whom you owe nothing, out of sheer altruism.
- In special cases, ignore any or all of these elements.

This proposed code could clearly benefit from additional dicta, but the flavor should be here, if not the entire recipe. One additional element that occurs to me immediately is that all transactions must be colored by the background, hangups, and perceptions of parties to the arrangement; sensitivity to these factors can distinguish the adroit manipulator from the blunderer.

To push this consideration of scientific transactions one step further, I have tried in Figure 8 to quantify some of the actions, recognizing that much more sophisticated approaches may exist and that few professionals have the time or inclination to keep a literal balance sheet anyway. Furthermore, the subjective assignment of points

Note: The suggested point values (ranging from 1 to 5) to be gained or lost are predicated on transactions between peers. They must be weighted if a colleague is junior or senior to you.

Action	Point value
Present lecture in colleague's course	1
Present several lectures in colleague's course so he/she can attend society meeting	4
Present seminar at colleague's institution—without honorarium	1
Agree to present paper at society session being convened by colleague	3
Agree to present invited paper at society symposium being organized by colleague	5
Agree to co-author paper with colleague (equal data contribution and equal writing responsibility)	1
Provide unpublished data to colleague for inclusion in his/her review paper	3
Agree to review and comment on colleague's rough draft of a scientific paper	3
Provide glowing letter of recommendation for colleague looking for a new job	1
Agree to read and comment on draft review paper or book chapter written by colleague	4
Accept marginal graduate student at personal request of colleague	5
Agree to review lengthy and marginal manuscript at request of journal editor	2
Accept invitation of colleague to act as co-editor of book with all contributed chapters by others	1
Accept invitation of colleague to contribute a chapter to a book for which he/she will be sole editor	5
As thesis committee member, sign approval form for thesis of colleague's student, even though thesis is marginal	5

FIGURE 8. Suggested point values for typical transactions among scientists.

for each action can be debated—but the *concept* is not trivial, since it concerns, ultimately, the way scientists allocate their precious professional hours.

Assignment of actual point values in the figure is clearly a subjective exercise; any numbers may be inserted, *provided* the donor and recipient agree on what they will be. Similarly, the weighting for stature in the field is highly subjective.

Questions that may occur to a casual reader of this material include: "What are the benefits of acquiring points?" or "What do scientists do with the points they gain?" or "How is a scientist with many points viewed differently from one in a deficit situation?" Answers to such questions are likely to be somewhat vague, since full codification and quantification of transactions in science have not yet been and may never be accomplished. In general, though, a substantial positive point score is indicative of a productive, involved, and energetic professional, whereas a persistently negative score tends to characterize the marginally productive and unconcerned scientist. A positive point balance during much of a career is a worthwhile goal for good professionals; peers and colleagues are usually well aware of those with such balances and turn to them in times of need. Colleagues also tend to respond more quickly and more thoroughly to any requests from those with consistently positive balances.

All this talk of point balances does not imply, however, that interactions among scientists are all coldly calculated, with every move being automatically entered in some great computer in the sky. There is abundant altruism and sharing in science, without thought of refunds or profits. The nurturing of graduate students, the supportive reviews of colleague's papers, the effective multidisciplinary research project—all are examples of mutual concern about the pleasure and progress of other professionals.

COMPROMISES IN SCIENCE

The transactional aspects of science blend easily into the great gray area of *compromises* in science—the small daily prostitutions that are part of the existence of most practitioners, except for the fanatically pure ones. Such compromises rarely invade the real substance of science—research and the presentation of research results—but they do abound in all the interpersonal compartments of professional existence. Some examples of the kinds of decisions that involve compromises are: dealing with marginal ethical practices of colleagues, backing off from a controversy, participating in selection of new junior faculty members, and contributing to tenure or promotion decisions about average faculty colleagues. It is easy to take an inflexible no-exceptions approach, but "the system" does not function well this way, and needless stress for you and pain for others can be consequences.

Take as an example a case that I have used repeatedly in discussions on ethics and in more formal presentations on interpersonal strategies in science:

Three years ago, you published a good review paper in your specialty. You now pick up a new textbook, by an author un-

known to you, that contains a number of paragraphs—even entire pages—that sound familiar. Checking your earlier paper, you find that the textbook author has paraphrased *your work, changing a few words here and there, but keeping the same sequence of thoughts and manner of presentation, and even most of the same literature citations—all without credit to you.*

What do you do? Do you run to the book publisher screaming plagiarism? Do you accept the usurpation of your material as a compliment, since someone has at least read it and found it quotable (even if without giving credit)? Do you smile and dismiss the incident as another example of marginal ethics? Or none of the above?

Clearly, the ethical standards of that author approach a zone that must be labeled questionable, but the book is published, it may never see a second printing, and the matter may not be worth the unpleasantries that could result. Most respondents, when confronted with this as a hypothetical case, opted for dismissing the transgressions, since the original paper had been published, and fleeting credit was derived at that time. A few elected to write a letter to the miscreant author, indicating awareness of the abuse—but these respondents tended to be less experienced in the everyday realities of scientific careers.

Consider another example:

You have agreed to develop joint data and to publish with a more senior colleague in a related discipline. The lab work and the analyses seemed to be proceeding well—almost too well at times. Then, completely by chance, you discover that your colleague (who is also a personal friend) has been "trimming" his data—ignoring results of some experiments that did not fit expected patterns. He is now following the original agreement and is pressing for preparation of the joint manuscript, of which you are projected to be junior author. Once your initial consternation has subsided, what courses of action are available to you? Should you confront him with your evidence, hoping for a reasonable explanation? Should you withdraw from the project, claiming pressure of other commitments? Should you allow the project to drag on and die naturally, insisting that more experiments must be done in your area of the project, but never quite doing them? Or none of the above?

This is a case in which purists among my respondents leaped in, demanding confrontation, to ensure the preservation of scientific integrity, and to hell with friendship. Others, but only a small majority, favored less traumatic approaches (all, of course, indicated that the paper must not be published with joint authorship). A number of the respondents felt that the project should be allowed to dwindle and disappear and that future proposals for joint research, if any, should be screened more carefully. Some felt that any public disclosure of ethical lapses by the colleague would serve no useful purpose, but a few felt that he should somehow be warned, very delicately, about ethically appropriate research practices.

Consider one more case:

Your institution provides a forum for faculty comments and recommendations about promotion and tenure decisions that affect other colleagues. As an Associate Professor with tenure, you are expected to participate. This year, an aggressive, ar-

ticulate young Assistant Professor is eligible for a tenure decision. Her research has been funded; it involves joint projects with young colleagues in two other countries. Her teaching is adequate, but she is often away from the campus for research reasons. She has been applying for positions elsewhere, but no suitable job has materialized. You have disagreed with her sharply and repeatedly at departmental seminars, and you view her as a pompous if very bright young woman, more concerned with self-advancement than with science, and with scant loyalty to the university. You are in a position to influence a tenure decision about her, and your intense dislike for her is well known. The faculty expects you to comment. What is your course of action?

I suppose sweet reasonableness should be the rule in this case, even though it is tempting to make a negative response and it is hard to eliminate personal prejudices at times like these. The real issue is the well-being of the university and how she fits its long-term needs. There seem to be few real strengths in her credentials or performance, so the reasonable response should probably be low-key, but recommending denial of tenure. This of course renders you susceptible to claims of bias, so the safe position would probably be one of near-neutrality.

These few pages on transactions and compromises get us a little closer to reality in the practice of science. Idealism is often supplanted by pragmatism, objectivity is bent or abandoned in favor of personal considerations, and a dynamic balance is preserved throughout the system. All this reinforces the obvious—that science is a *human* activity, performed by imperfect people with their own values and needs. Some reasonable structure must be maintained to ward off chaos, so the recognition and acceptance of transactions and compromises in the people relationships of science are critical to its well-being.

SCIENTISTS FOR HIRE: CONSULTING EXPERIENCES FOR NEW SCIENTISTS

This chapter seems thus far to have focused on the negative side of science, so we might as well continue the trend by considering a specialized area in which compromises are probably the most common—*consulting activities*. Academic salaries in American universities have been and still are abominable (with a few notable exceptions, usually for more senior faculty members at selected institutions). This condition of deprivation can lead quickly to decisions to augment salaries with consulting fees, if the scientist is in a field, such as molecular biology, computer applications, or high-energy physics, in which expertise is a marketable commodity. Most universities recognize that need, not by raising salaries, but by allowing their faculty up to one day a week (or some stated percentage of their time) for consulting activities. This allowance keeps good people on the staff, whereas they might otherwise defect to a better-paying industrial job, even though their primary interests are academic.

In examining the consulting situations that new scientists may encounter, some seem more common than others; they include:

1. A one-shot problem-solving episode, in which the scientist is hired, usually on a per diem basis, to

contribute to solution of a critical problem or to prepare a report.

2. A continuing arrangement, at a stated price, in which the scientist is available at specific or irregular times to apply his/her expertise to company problems.

3. A continuing arrangement, in return for a salary, stock, and/or stock options, in which the scientist forms a permanent part of the core of expertise on which the company depends.

4. Participation by the scientist, for a stated annual salary, in the business affairs of the company, as an officer or member of the board of directors, in addition to his/her role as scientific advisor.

5. Resignation from an academic position, to devote full time to consulting or to form an independent consulting company.

Depending on the scientist's inclinations and financial needs, involvement in consulting may stop at any of these stages; in general, steps (1) and (2) are by far the most common and the least controversial.

A basic problem, never far from the surface in consulting work, but rarely discussed openly, is an *ethical* one—revolving around the question: "How can a scientist remain impartial and objective in an environment in which a particular point of view is being pressed and in which he/she is being *paid* by an organization that may have financial interest in that point of view (pro or con)?" Solutions to the problem are rarely totally satisfactory; most scientists cling to ethical conduct in their research and in reporting results, but some are more ''liberal'' in *conclusions* reached and *interpretations* made on the basis of those results (and the results obtained by others). It is almost a truism that scientists, when confronted with identical data sets, may reach quite different conclusions or may interpret the data differently, depending on personal experiences and unacknowledged biases. The question of ethics arises only when some consultants repeatedly and consistently interpret data in favor of the viewpoints and interests of their employers. Even then, suspicions of unethical conduct are difficult to prove.

Enough horror stories exist about unethical practices of consultants, however, to suggest that abuses do occur. One senior faculty member, during discussion of the problem, listed those that he had encountered first-hand during his career (which had included a number of consulting arrangements):

- Scientists who actually *lie* at hearings.
- Scientists who slant conclusions to fit their own personal views or those of their employers.
- Scientists who accept jobs that require them to develop a basis for one side or another in legal cases.
- Scientists who are pure but can't get their data and conclusions into the record because of prejudices of the commission chairman or because of legal maneuvering by opposition lawyers.
- Scientists who become embroiled deliberately in cases with political overtones.

Now, admittedly, this listing emphasizes the negative aspects of consulting, probably drawn from single

events. The list points out some of the abuses, but it ig-
nores the positive contributions of many good scientists
who supply information on a fee basis.

---

*An excellent example of the ethical morass that some consult-
ing assignments may lead to was reported recently with some
enthusiasm by the news media. A major scientific consulting
firm was given contracts by a large East Coast city sewerage
authority to investigate possible effects of its sewer outfalls on
marine life. Good people with appropriate specialties participated in an adequately funded three-year field and experimental
program. The results of the multidisciplinary study were
equivocal; clear legal evidence for damage to marine populations
and their habitats was minimal, despite some statistical differences when normal and degraded sites were compared.*

*Some scientists employed by regulatory agencies were care-
fully doubtful about the interpretations of findings, although
they did not dispute the study design or the validity of the
results obtained. Agency scientists were joined by university
environmental biologists serving as expert witnesses during the
public hearings that followed publication of the report.*

*Lawyers for environmental activist groups disputed the
credibility of some investigators hired by the consulting company, and lawyers for the sewerage authority retaliated by ques-
tioning the credentials of some of the university experts in the
narrow area under question. The regulatory agencies involved
reached a foregone conclusion—that more data were required
before a clear finding of damage could be substantiated—but in
the process, scientific reputations were called into question and
a number of relatively junior scientists were thrust into a legal arena for which they had had little preparation.*

After consideration of a number of such case histories and discussion of work-related issues with scientific consultants, it was possible to assemble some rather nebulous guidelines relevant especially to junior professionals who may see consulting as one career objective:

- Credibility as a productive scientist is one basic requirement for successful consulting, since people with contract money to spend naturally want the best for their dollars.
- On-the-job training, serving as a temporary apprentice to a successful consultant (either one who is the entire company or one who manages the work of others), is probably the best entry-level strategy.
- Two critical competencies needed for success in consulting are writing skills and the capacity to assimilate and synthesize masses of data quickly and logically.
- Decisions about consulting as a vocation, full-time or part-time, should be based in part on examination of personal attitudes toward the ethical pressures involved—such as nondisclosure (also nonpublication) and the palatability of advocacy positions that match those of the employer.
- Consultants must expect serious review and criticism of their findings by colleagues, some of whom may assume adversary positions. Because of this, the science involved should be as flawless as possible and as complete as funding permits.
- Consultants, probably even more than academic or government colleagues, must be careful about not extending conclusions beyond what can be

supported by available data, despite pressures from employers, lawyers, or the news media to do so.

• Consultants should have (or should acquire) some smattering of legal training, since their opinions may be financially significant to employers and disputed by others—to the extent of legal proceedings in which consultants act as expert witnesses, sometimes in adversary roles with other scientists.

• Consultants must spend appreciable chunks of time in search of new contracts, especially if consulting is their principal means of support (this is not quite so critical a matter for university-based scientists).

Despite the pitfalls, good scientists can provide a much-needed service (at a price) to organizations that lack the necessary expertise or really want an unbiased outside opinion from credible professionals. Consulting can be a rough, competitive business, though, with maximum demands on the knowledge, ingenuity, and communication skills of the practitioner.

CHAPTER 12

THE PROFESSIONAL FACADE
OF SCIENCE

Conference Etiquette for Junior Scientists; Orchestrating Professional Conferences and Symposia—An Art Form; Conference Games for Female Scientists; Emerging as a "Key Figure" in Scientific Gatherings

INTRODUCTION

Scientific research has been variously defined, but its essence is the production and publication of new information leading to greater understanding of man and his environment. Understanding, of course, includes the evolution of concepts and principles and the accretion of evidence to support them. All this is important, but at times dreadfully dull and pedestrian. To permit escape from the daily routine, and to encourage admixture with colleagues, the scientific community has created its own elaborate social structure of society meetings, workshops, symposia, and conferences on regional, national, and international levels. These gatherings, which I call "the professional facade of science," offer opportunities to present new findings in critical forums—findings that may be reported dutifully in the news media. The real value of scientific meetings, though, extends far beyond information exchange into areas of personal interactions among colleagues. It is here, at the personal level, that much of the meaningful action takes place—not in the dim, half-filled or sometimes crowded session rooms.

Because professional gatherings are such a significant component of the infrastructure of science, it seems worthwhile, in this book aimed at the introductory-level scientist, to elaborate on at least some of the kinds of meetings and the efforts required for their success. Over many decades, an almost infinite number of approaches have been explored in attempts to improve formats and levels of communication. Some progress has been made, especially with the appearance of professional meeting-organizing companies, and conferences seem to run more smoothly with each passing decade. Improvements are still possible, though, and occasionally a new idea or approach is tried.

Since many of the nitties concerned with organizing scientific sessions and meetings were discussed in *Winning the Games Scientists Play*—the first volume in this trilogy—we are free in this volume and this chapter to explore a few newer and undoubtedly more interesting concepts concerned with professional meetings, expanding on the material presented in the earlier publication.

CONFERENCE ETIQUETTE
FOR JUNIOR SCIENTISTS

One criterion of proper development for the emergent scientist is his record of participating in professional conferences of various kinds, from meetings of state academies of science to international symposia. Probably the most common and most valuable entry-level kind of participation is the annual meeting of a national scientific society. During such a meeting, occasional visits to session rooms can be interspersed with corridor discussions and evening "field trips"—all producing what are easily some of the pleasantest interludes in scientific careers.

Scientific meetings should be relaxing, low-stress episodes (unless, of course, you are giving a paper). Attendance can be more pleasurable as well as more profitable for newcomers if some attention is given to common-sense etiquette. The meeting is, after all, a social event, so some operational guidelines might be expected to apply—and they do. Among the most useful, in my opinion, are these:

- Get on the program. Present a good paper or perform well at the poster session.
- During discussions of papers in your specialty, try to make some meaningful statement or ask a cogent question—anything that signals your presence and active participation; anything that gives you face and brain recognition; anything that even briefly identifies you and gives a clue about your

capabilities. But—do not do so at great length, or too obtrusively, or in any way negatively.

- When in the session room, stay awake by all means, but also be alert and receptive to interactions with peers or other participants.
- Always take along to the session room some letters to write or a manuscript to edit, as well as a tiny flashlight—to use during particularly dull or unintelligible presentations in a darkened room.
- Many papers presented at scientific society meetings are wastes of time and are often on the program merely to ensure that the author's attendance will be approved and funded. You will hate yourself later for sitting dumbly through such papers. Don't do it too often. Read abstracts, then go and talk with someone in the corridor.
- Talk to people at every opportunity, even if the ice-breaking effort is painful and difficult at first and against your natural reclusive tendencies. Don't stand mutely at the periphery of large groups waiting for someone to notice you. No one will.
- Never, never open a conversation at a scientific meeting with "I'll bet you don't remember me" or "Do you remember me?" or any similar stupid statement or question. State your name clearly, even if you have met the person several times, and let the recognition come from him (if at all). Otherwise, only embarrassment results if the person really doesn't remember you, but doesn't want to admit it, or remembers your face but not

your name, or (worse still) doesn't remember you and says so.

- Scientific meetings are always pleasanter if they are attended with a compatible colleague, with whom you can meet occasionally, without restricting contacts to that person. This is especially true of some of the giant and increasingly impersonal meetings of national professional societies.

- On receiving the final meeting program at registration, identify a half day when the titles of papers seem particularly uninteresting, and begin planning an external field trip with colleagues— preferably in a rental car and to a site with historic or other interest (e.g., Disney World, Grant's Tomb, Tijuana, Yosemite). Let nothing interfere with the plan, and if necessary expand it to occupy a full day. Unless external contacts of this kind are pursued vigorously, a meeting can degenerate into little more than long hours spent in darkened function rooms of a huge downtown hotel, in a city unseen except during the taxi ride from and to the airport. Let that be someone else's meeting—not yours!

- At least once during every meeting, invite a moderate-size group of colleagues (10–20) to your hotel room for cocktails and other refreshments (which you provide). This can be very early or very late in the evening, but is best carried off early in the meeting (though not in conflict with the general reception/banquet). In anticipation of this gathering, register for as large a room as your finances will permit (industry scientists should consider renting suites, since their expense accounts are so generous). Provisions can be brought to the meeting, if you are driving, or bought at inflated prices at shops near the meeting hotel, if you travel by plane.

• Always consider a pre- or postmeeting visit with a colleague located in or near the convention city or on the way to or from the meeting. An invitation from him to present a seminar could give the stopover some legitimacy, but do it anyway. We see too little of colleagues who are friends during professional careers.

In looking back over these guidelines, it may seem that the scientific component of the meeting is relatively insignificant—and this is a good perception. Scientific conferences are primarily and predominantly *social* functions and should be approached from that perspective. The *science* that is conveyed and discussed in formal sessions of the conference may be relevant and exhilarating, but it should never be allowed to become the sole objective of attendance.

ORCHESTRATING PROFESSIONAL CONFERENCES AND SYMPOSIA—AN ART FORM

It is not unusual for scientists, even for relatively junior people, to be asked to serve on organizing committees for a spectrum of meetings, from a regional workshop to a national society meeting to an international symposium. The request probably must be considered an "honor," but acceptance implies commitment to a complex job, especially if physical arrangements for the meeting are included as well as the scientific program. Service on an organizing committee is a part of growing up in science, it is a learning experience as well as a consumer of time, and it is best performed as early in a professional career as possible.

Some societies have developed printed guidelines for meeting organizers, but often these are limited to instructions for session chairmen, instructions for judges of "best scientific paper" awards, or instructions for visual-aid preparation. Many other aspects of organizing are left to the ingenuity and foresight of the committee or to the dim recollections of those unfortunates who have served before.

This is not a good state of affairs. On the shelves of scientific libraries all across the country, there should be a standard reference book entitled *Organizing Professional Meetings* and filed next to *American Men and Women of Science*. The book would take members of an organizing committee step by step and day by day from the first informal discussion about an idea for a conference through to publication of the proceedings, listing all the nitties and pitfalls, with entire chapters devoted to such topics as "Registration," "The Ideal Program Structure," "Coffee Breaks," "Spouses' Programs," "Receptions" (maybe an entire book on this subject alone), "Banquet Speakers," "Keynote Speakers"—and on and on.

Extracted from the modest quantity of printed and other information that I have seen, some principles seem to have overriding value, especially for organizing national and international conferences. I have arbitrarily selected thirteen of them that do not seem to have received enough emphasis in other places:

- The theme or central concept of a meeting, be it a workshop, symposium, special session at a society meeting, international conference, minisymposium, or whatever, should be developed fully by a small group who will function (with some additional members) as the organizing committee. The first assembly of this group is critical to the success of the venture, since all the broad guidelines should be stated and recorded. Ingredients include a convener (who may or may not turn out to be the general chairman of the meeting), the right mix of organizing committee members (some young and energetic, some older but recognized in the field), a program in which all members of the committee have something to gain (visibility as session chairmen, platforms to express points of view, ability to select friends as invited speakers, or permission to try some innovative approaches). The initial meeting of the group should be held in a faculty dining room or the executive dining room of an industrial research and development organization (depending on the positions held by committee members). Before coffee is served, the committee should have (1) decided whether the proposed meeting is go or no-go; (2) roughed out the entire meeting, including a detailed statement of the theme, a tentative list of key speakers, and a provisional agenda; and (3) discussed funding requirements and sources. The convener will prepare, within a week, a follow-up summary of the planning session, with a timetable for all the preliminary activities.

- If the budget for the meeting will permit, an outside professional meeting-organizing company should be hired to take responsibility for physical arrangements, to permit scientists to focus their attention on the scientific program.
- Very early in the organizing process, invitations should be extended to the core group of speakers and chairmen who will help ensure the scientific success of the meeting. Members of the core group are keynote speaker, invited session speakers, session chairmen, luncheon and banquet speakers, panelists, and conference summarizer. These form the basic structure; other participants fill in the squares.
- Probably the best approach (again dependent on the projected meeting budget) is to have as many key roles as possible and to offer each one a token financial inducement (especially for international meetings), with the promise that if attendance and registration permit, the amount will be increased. The full tab should be paid —without quibble— for keynote and banquet speakers. Make sure that every core group member understands the amount of the honorarium, whether or not registration is to be prepaid, and what the extent of editing responsibilities will be after the meeting.
- Whenever possible, select members of "the club" for key roles, get early commitments from them, and feature their names in promotional literature for the meeting. Commitments for key slots are obtained most readily if early letters of invitation

come from friends or from recognizable members of the club.

- If the format of the meeting permits, state the intention of publishing the proceedings (or at least the invited papers) as a hardcover book within one year—and carry through. Some of the initial funding and part of the registration fee should be set aside as an inducement to publishers. The one-year deadline is feasible only if authors submit final copies of manuscripts at the time of the meeting. (At a recent meeting in Australia, I encountered the ultimate: A hardcover book containing all invited papers was distributed *at the time of registration*.)

- So-called "multidisciplinary" or "interdisciplinary" sessions at scientific meetings should be approached with great caution. Meeting organizers seem persistently overoptimistic about drawing together participants from two or more disciplines, even if the session program should be attractive to all. The reality is that specialists attend sessions in their own fields—so water resource engineers should not be expected to appear at competing sessions on biological effects of pollution, and biochemists from pharmaceutical companies should not be expected to attend a session on aquaculture. In my experience, interdisciplinary sessions work only marginally if no other concurrent session is scheduled, and even then, meeting attendees may stay in the halls, go to the cocktail lounge, or go sightseeing, rather than attend a session outside their specialty.

- Sometimes, and especially in the closing hours of society meetings, session attendance is so poor that chairmen wonder whether to proceed or cancel. The only rule that I have heard enunciated for such situations is that if the audience outnumbers the speakers at the start of the session, then the show goes on; if it does not, then the session should be converted to a round-table discussion, with speakers as participants, but including the precious few members of the audience as well. Informal rather than formal talks can be given, and any new arrivals who wander in can be incorporated into the circle.

- Organizing committees should be conservative about the intrusion of ad hoc meetings on the regular agenda. Often, narrow special-interest groups will propose workshops or other gatherings that conflict with scheduled sessions—a no-no. Often, too, the same narrow special-interest groups will attempt to use the meeting as a vehicle for making some public statement on activist issues—also a no-no.

- Organizing committees must not be disheartened by nit-pickers and nay-sayers, who surface in every scientific meeting, particularly during coffee breaks. These people *always* find problems with the organization of any meeting, regardless of how carefully it has been planned. They pick out minor inconveniences—the coffee break is too crowded, the discussion following paper presentation is too short, the schedule is allowed to slip, the accoustics are poor—and on and on. Ignore them!

- Meeting organizers should not be dismayed by average or poor performances by key speakers. Even though programs are built around these stars, they may for a variety of reasons be stunningly mediocre or they may "bomb." Whatever the outcome, organizers should accept the actuality with aplomb, after taking their best shot at the selection of speakers.
- Conference organizers should recognize the great variability in perspectives on the meeting and in meeting activities from one participant to another. Consider how different the meeting is for:
  1. *A society officer*, for whom the meeting consists of marathon sessions of the board of directors, participation at the opening session, presentation of a report at the business meeting, a brief pause to listen to a few papers, and cocktail parties.
  2. *The superelite*—the inner circle of club members—who give the keynote speeches, get invited to faculty clubs for meals and to embassy receptions (at some international conferences), give television interviews in spacious lounges or media rooms of the meeting hotel, but rarely enter the session rooms.
  3. *Senior members* of the society, for whom the meeting consists of corridor conversations and long lunches with peers, occasional attendance at the scientific sessions, and evening visits with old friends who live in or near the conference city.
  4. The *free-rangers*, who use the meeting as a convenient moon base for frequent forays to tourist

attractions, nightclubs, casinos, or distant points of quasi-scientific interest.

5. *New members* of the society, with their own circle of post-Ph.D. friends, for whom the meeting consists of stressful final preparation for a presentation of a scientific paper, setup and attendance at poster sessions, prolonged technical discussions with cohorts from other institutions, and evenings at local discos with a small group of friends from the conference.

Even for midcareer scientists, any meeting may be totally different for each individual, depending on sex, gregariousness, membership in "the club," presence of spouse, extent of involvement in the society, and a host of other factors. "The Meeting" thus becomes many simultaneous and often only slightly overlapping meetings, built around a framework of scientific sessions and planned events, but not dominated by them.

• Members of organizing committees would be well advised to pay great attention to the size and location of the obligatory "reception" or cocktail party. Public exhibition facilities are often selected for large receptions during scientific meetings. Such affairs are often supported in part by the conference city, and they can be very elaborate buffets with abundant liquid refreshments. They tend to be memorable for a variety of reasons; the memories usually far outlast the specifics of the meeting itself.

I can remember well a summer meeting of a Zoological Congress, when the reception was held in the Washington Zoo. The bar was set up in the snake house, and a truly overwhelming buffet was laid out in the elephant house. Unfortunately, the fly population in the elephant house was also overwhelming; it quickly dominated the pastries, the meats, the fruits, and everything—excluding all but the hungriest zoologists.

Two receptions in public aquaria also remain in my memory. One, in Seattle, was cleverly arranged in tiers down a circular ramp descending through spectacular exhibits. The buffet became progressively more elaborate during the descent, from sandwiches and chips at the surface to king crab and roast beef at the lowermost level. Unfortunately, many of the participants never got to the lowest level (siphoned off by exhibits, potato chips, and discussions with friends).

Another recent giant cocktail party at the Vancouver Aquarium disclosed a new technique. In a venue consisting of a series of circular ramps descending from coelocanth to killer whale, the hors d'oeuvres were arranged on large wheeled carts that were pushed continuously and briskly up and down the ramps. Participants had to be nimble to partake of the moveable feast. Food could be snatched as the carts went by, and some vehicles with choice goodies were followed by a swarm of participants like seagulls behind a fishing vessel.

While I do not mean to belabor unduly the concept of the beloved "reception," it would seem only fitting to conclude the discussion with a few observations on national and international character traits of this most stable and enjoyable feature of scientific conferences. Allowing for some slight variability, look for these standard methods:

- In the *United States*, look for great mounds of food available in numerous locations in the reception hall as soon as the doors open—but don't expect second servings and do be prepared to pay for liquid refreshments at a so-called "cash bar."
- In *Canada*, the event takes on a little more decorum, with beer and wine only, and with no food in sight until after the obligatory speeches of welcome. Then expect delicacies of distinctively Canadian origin.
- In *Japan*, Western-style receptions are rare, but if they occur, expect elaborately and elegantly presented seafoods with Western-style liquors (especially Japanese Scotch whisky). The more customary reception, but for smaller groups, is an elaborate sit-down meal with uncountable courses—all exquisite.
- In *Poland* (and a few other Communist countries including the Soviet Union), even in harsh times of unavailability of almost anything from ham to toilet paper, receptions for foreigners are characterized by a sudden blossoming of delicacies not seen in local markets for years (even decades), augmented by oceans of vodka and other national beverages.

CONFERENCE GAMES FOR FEMALE SCIENTISTS

The presence of female scientists is of course an ever-expanding feature of professional meetings. Here are a few premises for women:

- Such gatherings are primarily *social* events rather than technical ones (the technical component is the necessary facade).
- Social encounters need not be sexual; there is always a wide selection of pleasant group activities that need not be in any way physical.
- Socializing among scientists is inadequate on a day-to-day basis, so professional meetings supply much-needed if too-infrequent occasions for it.
- The pleasures of group activities are always increased when both sexes participate.

While the mere presence of excellent female scientists does much by itself to improve any meeting, active social roles assumed by both men and women can make the event a memorable one. Careful study of socially oriented women scientists at many meetings, as well as prolonged discussions with a few of the best, have produced a random list of admonitions, suggestions, and dicta that may be useful (or may be totally misleading) to almost any female professional who attends a conference:

- Male scientists are professionals, but most of them have the normal interests and urges of human beings. Expect clumsy passes from inept male scientists or smoother ones from ept ones, especially in the dying moments of small-group cocktail parties at scientific conferences. Be firm and definite in your position while trying to maintain a calm demeanor.
- At professional meetings, develop (and even be a ringleader or tour guide for) a core of companions

of both sexes for occasional small-group evening entertainment—but don't restrict contacts during the day to members of that group, since conferences offer great opportunities to meet other colleagues.

- Travel by car to and from national or regional meetings often involves a mixed group. Guidelines about who pays and how much, where the group stays if the trip is extensive, who drives, and other details should be discussed in advance. It is important in attending a meeting with that kind of group for each person to retain independence of action and movement during the meeting, as far as possible or desired.

- Most conferences schedule banquets or receptions for some evenings, but other evenings are free. Seize one of those free evenings to give an invitation-only cocktail party of your own—in your hotel room after dinner. Expect to incur the displeasure of the hotel management and guests in adjacent rooms, but do it anyway.

- Officers and boards of directors of societies have their own social events during the meeting, in addition to the larger ones that include all participants. Some of these "enclave" events are not totally exclusive, and they can be elaborate and exciting, so it is worth a little special effort to gain entry to them (probably the best way is to know or to get to know one of the in group and to go as his/her guest).

- Avoid, by whatever means possible, the prospect or the actuality of a meal alone—especially an evening meal—in a hotel dining room. Any single person, and especially a single female, will be subjected to the usual unpleasantries—a tiny table in the corner or near the kitchen and waiters who are either impatient or invisible. Many people—and especially many male colleagues—at scientific meetings would welcome uncomplicated company at meals, but some are diffident about asking. Be aggressive.

A logical response to the emphasis in this section on female scientists—particularly after the entire Chapter 4 on "The Savvy Female Graduate Student"—could well be: "How is the *male* scientist at professional meetings so different, and where is a comparable sexist treatment of him in this book?" My defense, and it seems to be a reasonable one from a male perspective, is that *all* scientists can enjoy and profit from personal exchanges at conferences, but superimposed on these exchanges are special strictures, and opportunities, that apply more to females than to males.

EMERGING AS A "KEY FIGURE" IN SCIENTIFIC GATHERINGS

Scientists like to form temporary aggregates—be they society conferences, working group meetings, committee meetings, symposia, workshops, or any other assembly of more than two individuals. There is joy in participating in events such as these; there is more joy in being a leader or a principal actor in them. Sideline observers at enough of these gatherings soon recognize the members of a small elite group who emerge consistently as chairmen, session conveners, society officers, rapporteurs, executive committee members, invited speakers, keynote speakers—any and all of the visible and influential roles. A logical if somewhat naïve question, especially for the upwardly mobile new scientist to ask, is: "How did they get that way?" The routes are sometimes direct and sometimes convoluted, so it makes the most sense to offer some tentative generalizations:

- *Credibility as a professional* is again the foundation, the stepping stone, and the departure ramp for any proposed excursions beyond routine participation in scientific gatherings. Some roles, such as keynote or invited speaker, can be achieved only by this route; many others, such as session chairman or working group chairman, depend in part on credibility and in part on organizing skills.
- Professional societies usually have a stable core of active long-term members and it is from this group that *officers and members of boards of directors* are often drawn. There is some slow infusion of new blood into key jobs, normally beginning with the board of directors. Recruits to the elite circle are often drawn from the list of society members who have served on standing committees or in repeat performances as session chairmen—or sometimes from a pool of friends of current officers of the organization. Shortcuts in this system do occur, but they are rare. New scientists are best advised to select a few good national societies early in their careers, to present papers, and to volunteer for committee assignments (organizing

committee members work hard but get excellent visibility), to offer suggestions for special sessions (which they *may* be asked to chair), to meet and get to know as many society members as possible, to participate actively in discussions at scientific sessions and business meetings, and to be visible in ad hoc meetings held during the annual meeting. If most of these ground-level things are done well, then chairmanships (standing committees, sessions, organizing committees) may be offered, and eventually a niche on the ballot may be proposed by the nominating committee.

- Some professionals have "natural abilities" that almost automatically place them in leadership positions, especially in society committees. If some of the people who might be so identified are examined, common traits will be seen to include self-confidence, assertiveness, willingness to take risks, and ability to grow in the job. Some individuals in this category can be further classified as "tried and true but reluctant." These are good professionals with experience, who are willing to serve again in a crisis, and who do the job well if they elect to become involved. They often bring along new members who will serve as apprentices and who will be called on later because of that experience.

- Scientific societies are replete with "warm bodies" who enjoy the meetings, who are willing to serve on committees, and who will do the minimum expected of them. For those few willing to assume greater responsibilities and leadership roles, a common attitude, as expressed by the members, is often: "Go to it, and more power to you."

- *Chairmanships of standing committees or working groups* are choice jobs for capable scientists. They provide visibility (in presenting reports and other documents, such as position papers or lists of recommendations), and they provide a vehicle for demonstrating administrative and organizing skills. Furthermore, tenure in such roles tends to be long-term, with potential for significant impact on the planning and future course of the organization. Some standing committees or working groups actually address issues of importance to *science* as well as to the *organization,* and these are undoubtedly the most satisfying to many professionals. Such groups may have extended lifespans, during which they meet regularly or exchange views by correspondence; they usually focus on single issues and often produce a sequence of definitive documents (protocols, advisories, position papers, recommendations). The documents may well form the basis for action by the parent organization. Enthusiastic participation in these groups is a source of pleasure for many who become involved, and chairing a standing committee or working group can be a legitimate item in the list of career objectives for good professionals.
- *Chairmanships of ad hoc committees* can also provide stimulating experiences for good scientists. Requisites include organizing abilities, sincere and expressed interest in the objectives of the committee, skill in interacting with colleagues, and previous

experience as a contributing member of diverse
committees with other objectives. Effective committee chairmen thus represent an amalgam of
background and expertise, overlaid with acquired
skills in guiding small-group meetings to productive end points (usually the preparation of a definitive report). Committee chairmanships are usually
appointive—that is, the society president or the institution director designates the chairman and
states the objectives of the group. Beyond this, the
success or failure of the committee depends to a
large extent on the skill of the designated leader,
especially if he has authority to select committee
members. During the often subjective process of
picking a chairman, the appointing authority normally sifts through a number of determining factors, not the least of which are track records of
candidates in carrying out similar assignments, degree of familiarity of candidates with the issues to
be addressed, and (to a lesser extent) compatibility of views of candidates with those of the appointing authority.

• On the technical side of any meeting program are
visible and highly desirable roles as *invited speaker,
symposium speaker, keynote speaker, luncheon speaker,
banquet speaker,* or *meeting summarizer.* Those
selected for the choice slots have usually followed
the long, difficult route of sustained excellence as
participants in poster sessions, contributors to
scientific sessions, and producers of significant
new information. Shortcuts are extremely rare, although exceptional innovative research may

shorten the period spent in the trenches of session papers before emergence as a key speaker. The emergence may be hastened, too, by acquiring some reputation as a good speaker—with impeccable diction, enthusiasm, memorable visuals, logical presentations, and even a touch of humor laid on. Outstanding skill as a public speaker is almost entirely the result of careful preparation and extensive experience—and, as such, is within the capabilities of most professionals who are willing to exert the effort.

- Still on the technical side, an invitation to participate in or (better still) to help organize an *international conference or symposium* can be a great boost to a scientific career and, if handled well, can be the window to an entirely new dimension of science. Most of the industrialized nations of the world number exceptional professionals among their populations; the close cooperation required to set up an international meeting permits the development of good contacts and even friendships. Additionally, vigorous participation in one such event often leads to requests from foreign counterparts for involvement in subsequent conferences or symposia, or even for development of joint research projects. Usually, access to the foreign scene is a consequence of outstanding performances in science at the national level; credibility acquired at home becomes an export commodity for competent scientists.

There are, of course, other routes to international science. Reception and care of visiting professionals on exchange fellowships or government grants can lead to reciprocal visits to their countries. Also, service as scientific advisor to an international commission or council (United Nations, World Health Organization, and many others) can provide visibility and opportunity for interaction with good foreign scientists who are serving in similar capacities. It should be emphasized that contacts of any kind with foreign professionals should be expanded upon promptly, before perceptions of the mutual benefits of continued communication and cooperation dissipate.

- In addition to the key roles already considered, whether in national or international gatherings, some meeting-related *specialized functions* can be performed well by selected individuals. One of the most welcomed at many meetings is the ''unofficial social director,'' with a reputation for seeking out excellent restaurants or clubs and making arrangements for evening events in those locations—often complete with special menus, entertainment, and transportation. His counterpart may specialize in seeking out and making arrangements for small-group visits to places of historic or scientific interest, apart from the regular tours planned by the organizing committee. Still other colleagues may organize small-group visits to the opera, to a ballet performance, or to a play. One of the most popular of this breed of social directors (for male attendees at least) assembles a short list of the best nightclubs and gambling houses in the meeting city and acts as guide for an evening of distraction from the concerns of science. While these social roles may not be direct routes to the society presidency, they do provide visibility, and they greatly enhance the pleasures of meeting participation.

In all these approaches to the phenomenon of emerging as a principal actor on the scientific stage, two common factors exist: *increasing credibility in science per se* and *competent performance in supporting roles at levels below those of the lead figures*. When combined, these factors make acquisition of the prizes—the key or leadership positions in assemblages of professionals—much more likely to occur.

The topics aggregated in this chapter under the title "The Professional Facade of Science" are obviously highly selected aspects of the much larger subject of extralaboratory activities of scientists. We have touched on conferences and other forums, mostly from an organizational point of view; we mentioned very briefly the role of female scientists in such gatherings, and then we examined (fleetingly) the role of "key figures" of scientific groups.

Professional meetings clearly constitute an important part of the social infrastructure of science. Properly organized and led, they provide welcome interludes away from the laboratory and classroom, and they permit scientists to indulge in soul-soothing and stimulating exchanges with colleagues, inside and outside the session rooms. The meetings can have various formats, but all of them have a common feature—they are vehicles for technical and personal exchanges among productive professionals.

CHAPTER 13

CREDIBILITY

Principal Components of Scientific Credibility; The "Matthew Effect" and Credibility; Credibility and Grant Support

Scientists are reputed to thirst for many things—recognition for significant contributions to understanding, academic status, pay increases, tenure, research grants, larger offices and laboratories, love, and sex (not necessarily in that order of priority). One item high on every want-list, but less tangible than some of the preceding, is *credibility as a professional*. Credibility resists precise definition, but includes elements of most of the following:

- Demonstrated and sustained productivity in specific subject-matter areas.
- Completion of work that is solid and substantive and is recognized as such by colleagues.
- Membership in a core group of contributors to progress in a specialty area.

- Authorship of creative reviews and/or a definitive book in a specialty area.
- Recognition as a critical analyst or synthesizer of data from diverse sources.
- Contributions to professional community activities (e.g., societies, symposia, workshops) as organizer or participant.
- Contributions to conceptual advances in a specialty area.
- Responsiveness to requests to present contributions (e.g., seminars, symposium papers, reviews, overviews, keynote speeches).
- Name recognition among peers for scientific contributions.
- Published papers that are read early on by first-year graduate students interested in that specialty area.
- Published papers that are read sooner or later by graduate students preparing for comprehensive examinations.
- Published papers that are read, digested, and assimilated by colleagues in a specialty area.

The hard question that is always asked about successful professionals—in this case scientists with credibility—is: "How, really, did they get that way, other than by satisfying most of the criteria just listed?" In looking at the careers of a number of credible practitioners, one finds a few hints:

- Credibility may be acquired by a record of perseverance when confronted by repeated frustrations—endurance and persistence in the face of repeated failures—but with final achievement of substantive results.

- Credibility may be acquired by accretion—the painfully slow but continuous and deliberate accumulation over a long period of facts to support or refute a concept, hypothesis, or idea.
- Credibility may be acquired by "success in small places," in which outstanding work can be done in museums, small private institutes, or small, little-known colleges, by scientists (such as systematists, anthropologists, or ecologists) working alone or in small enclaves.
- Credibility may be acquired by a "great leap forward," in which a brilliant definitive experiment or synthesis is presented to colleagues in all its beauty and is subsequently supported by the work and analyses of others.

Once acquired, credibility can be retained with less effort than was required to attain it. This curious phenomenon in science was explored thoroughly two decades ago by Robert K. Merton as "the Matthew effect in science"—defined by Merton (1968) as "...the accruing of greater increments of recognition for particular contributions to scientists of considerable repute and the withholding of such recognition from scientists who have not yet made their mark." The reference by Merton is to the Gospel according to St. Matthew: "For unto everyone that hath shall be given, and he shall have abundance; but from him that hath not shall be taken away even that which he hath." The reality of the phenomenon is demonstrated daily in countless ways: the grant proposal from a proven performer that is approved quickly, the ready acceptance by journals of manuscripts by leaders in their specialties, or the preferential treatment given in job placement to students of eminent scientists. The extensions of this concept of a "Matthew effect" as elaborated by Merton are also fascinating—particularly that eminent men of science not only *achieve personal excellence*, but also *evoke excellence in others*, their students in particular. Another is that for those who have achieved a high degree of credibility, peers and colleagues regard each scientific accomplishment as a prelude to greater ones, creating a social pressure that does not allow the achiever to remain content. Merton found little evidence for "repose at the top" in science, even though most of us today could point to individuals who achieved and then faded quickly from competition.

As a generalization, then, credible scientists work hard to maintain their status—which may be added to or subtracted from, almost like a checking account with a minimum balance requirement. Points are gained in numerous ways: publication of a significant new paper, a good thesis defense by a protégé, or a large grant award by the National Science Foundation. Points can be lost in just as many ways: bombing as a keynote speaker, rejection of a major paper by a key journal, publication of a mediocre book, or a declining record of productivity over time (often as a consequence of assuming administrative responsibilities). Incremental gains and losses, then, are the norm; radical changes in credibility status are rare and are usually the consequences of demonstrated fraud, extreme forms of midlife crisis, or dalliance with a lab technician.

Credibility among peers and colleagues is clearly a cherished lifetime accomplishment for good scientists and a worthwhile career objective for all professionals. In a less complex world, credible scientists would be universally accepted as such; in today's academic environment, however, this is not always the case. University administrators want more. To be known in a narrow discipline and to publish technical papers in national journals has become, to those arbiters, less than adequate if not accompanied by continuing research grants. Success in grantsmanship, with consequent financial gain to the institution in the form of overhead assessments on the grants, easily surpasses mere credibility in the absence of grants. The reality of this melancholy conclusion can be best seen when decisions about promotions and salary increases are made.

Scholarly publications are of course viewed as important, even by administrators, but *principally as tangible support for future grant applications, not as significant accomplishments in themselves.* This new criterion of worth tends to reduce the market value of excellent scientific publications, at least to that segment of the decision-making academic hierarchy involved in salary and tenure discussions. Does this mean that the list of elements leading to professional credibility, which was stated so confidently at the beginning of this chapter, is inadequate and should be amended to include "continuing success in negotiating research grants"? My answer, conservative as always, has to be "No." Credibility isn't bought with grants even though the availability of grant funds can greatly enhance productivity in some disciplines, by making it possible to hire assistants and to buy state-of-the-art equipment.

In any final analysis, though, credibility is in essence an *internal matter*—internal to the scientific community, the members of which are best able to assess it correctly and to reward colleagues who achieve it, and certainly internal to those excellent professionals who do achieve it.

CHAPTER 14

THE CHANGING ROLES
OF SCIENTISTS

Scientists in Public Places; Effects of "High Technology" on Scientists; Research Funding

The traditional public image of scientists includes such descriptors as:

- Dedicated to extreme objectivity in observations
- Carefully conservative in conclusions and generalizations
- Deliberately circumspect in public utterances
- Interested in elucidation of natural phenomena
- Insistent on experimental verification of observed events
- Concerned with evolution of concepts
- Reluctant to accept cause-and-effect relationships easily

This image is essentially correct; it portrays the scientist in a role that has produced remarkable advances in human knowledge, especially during this century. What the image fails to convey, however, is any sense of the dynamic nature of science and the urgency that scientists feel about the development of new information.

Events during the past several decades have propelled scientists into new areas of research, such as genetic manipulation, particle physics, and superconductors, and into new roles, such as greater involvement in public issues. These trends give every indication of accelerating and of carrying practitioners still further beyond their former laboratory-oriented universes.

Major changes have occurred and are occurring in the methodology and perspectives of scientists, including:

- Improved methods of data analysis, aided by advances in computer science.
- Exploration of the potentials of genetic engineering, in areas such as food production, elimination of hereditary diseases, and control of pathogens.
- Direct and immediate utilization of scientific findings in public controversies, such as those concerned with environmental degradation and population control.

In these and other emerging areas, a common factor is greater commitment of scientists to the *applications* of their research findings. Publication of research results is still an important goal, as it has always been, but more and more it is now augmented (even exceeded) by interest in patents and industrial applications and in use of data as a basis for decisions about current public issues or managing global resources. Scientists are and will be of increasing importance as *participants* in the decision-making process, as well as providers of data. Many complex current issues require that interpretations be made of and conclusions be drawn from large bodies of data—and this seems a proper function of trained people rather than laymen (without in any way suggesting that scientists should be final arbiters in issues with significant social, political, and economic components).

Thus, today's beginning scientist will be part of a seemingly rapid evolutionary era, probably as a direct participant, maybe even as a leader. In many specialty areas—ecology and public health, for example—the scientist will become more and more a public figure, with less and less time for quiet contemplation of research results before he must face a television camera or talk with a newspaper reporter. Many professionals thrive on this kind of attention to their findings, as an indication that they are doing "research that matters" and that their results and conclusions can be important to decisions that also have strong social, political, and economic overtones. Fortunately, for those less able to handle stress, there will always be, in every discipline, quieter areas in which good science can still be practiced (in biology, for example, we still need much more work in specialties such as systematics, physiology, and marine biology).

Probably some mention should also be made of changing roles for scientists in so-called "high-technology" research areas—new specialties, mostly in physics, biochemistry and genetics, that require extremely complex equipment and techniques. Some of the role changes already apparent are increased competitiveness among research groups, with coincident increases in secrecy until public pronouncements of findings are made; increased use of news media rather than professional journals to announce significant discoveries; competitive bidding for services of the best thinkers and technicians; detailed and restrictive contracts specifying terms of employment of professionals; maximum opportunity for consulting arrangements for academics with skills in critical areas; preoccupation with patentability and potential applications of research results; and the sudden expansion of a cadre of "scientist-entrepreneurs" who organize high-tech companies to perfect and market products of research.

Some positive role changes are also apparent. The high-technology growth areas offer exciting prospects for basic research in life processes—research that can lead to major advances in areas such as food production and disease control. To participate in this kind of science is immediately attractive to the well-trained and capable new scientist. Furthermore, unlike in most other research areas, good scientists encounter a sellers' market, with great demand for their services and offers of better-than-average compensation—and even an opportunity to control their own destinies by forming or joining venture companies.

A critical determinant of future research directions in science is of course research funding. In the past three and one-half decades, we have seen the unparalleled dominance of the Federal government in paying for research in the United States—starting, it seems, as a response to early consternation over "Sputnik" and subsequent Soviet advances in technology. That dominance of the Federal government in research support persists, and will probably continue, subject to some fluctuations according to the whims and attitudes of the administration in power. This means that decisions about funding for research are being made and will be made by politicians (aided by whatever scientific advisors they choose to listen to). Some observers view this concentration of control over research with alarm, objecting to the narrowness of vision and the mission orientation of government funding agencies. Others see government funding as the only solution to the needs of "big science" and to the uncertainties of private sector funding. Accepting the likelihood of the continuing presence of government in decisions about research grants, new scientists would be well advised to seize opportunities to understand the complex techniques of decision-making and control that have been elaborated in many funding agencies and to participate with great vigor in any scientific review and advisory procedures made available by those agencies. A relatively new role for scientists, which has developed in response to government dominance, was described earlier in this book as that of the "scientist-politician"—a credible professional who has learned how to deal effectively with systems of control and who can influence those systems to move in the best interests of the science community. For those scientists with the aptitude and interest, this role gives every indication of being even more important in the future.

The scientist of tomorrow, then, will be like his predecessors in conducting objective searches for new information and new or modified concepts leading to better understanding of natural phenomena. He may be different, though, in insisting on greater participation in decision-making, whether it be in connection with award of research grants or with public issues that need technical contributions. Coincident with increased participation in such decisions will be greater *responsibility* for the correctness of those decisions and greater *commitment* to effective communication of scientific information and viewpoints.

EPILOGUE

I've learned much about my colleagues through the exhausting research required to produce this volume. Most of all, I've learned that scientists are characterized by extreme variability—by resistance to being stuffed into neatly labeled pigeonholes. Still, they do have traits in common. Most are honest, intelligent, and inquisitive (but some are stubborn, insensitive, and stupid). Most are reasonable as human beings (but a few are impossible boors). Whatever their natures, they have shared with me, usually freely and graciously (but sometimes reluctantly or unwittingly), experiences and insights that have helped to shape this and the two earlier books in the trilogy.

One surprising conclusion from all this research is that scientists do accept the reality of interpersonal strategies that I and others call "games." Many, however, choose to retain amateur standing throughout their professional careers—learning slowly by experience while stumbling around in the thicket called "the system." I salute those dedicated individuals, but reserve my real respect for those who enter into the spirit of scientific games, who learn the rules early, and who play with vigor and enthusiasm—even adding creative nuances of their own to the existing body of knowledge. (Unfortunately, few players write down their new insights, so they are lost to later generations of scientists, unless rediscovered.)

This book, titled *Survival Strategies for New Scientists*, was aimed deliberately at the newcomers—the graduate students and postdocs—who must achieve quickly and well in their chosen specialties and who should acquire, just as quickly, an appreciation for the interpersonal components of science, if they are to sample its full riches. If I've tended to overuse the word "excellence," I've done so to imprint on beginners the importance of its connotations to all professionals. There are so many opportunities in science to do something so exceptionally well that observers have every right to be overwhelmed. I have heard symposium talks so exquisite as to bring a lump to the throat and lectures so brilliant as to bring tears to the eyes. Those responsible for inducing such honest emotions are to me the ultimate professionals, of the kind that most of us would like to be. We can try. We should try harder. Excellence is within reach for most of us, if we will but take Robert Browning's advice and reach a little beyond our grasp.

Let me close by repeating a confidence entrusted to me early in my career by a world-renowned invertebrate zoologist: "Sindermann," she said, "there are just three simple rules to follow to become a great scientist. The problem is—nobody knows what they are." This vacuum leaves all of us free to make up our own rules—which I have done profligately. For exit lines, my advice to new scientists can be condensed into six simple rules:

1. Establish *credibility* by *doing research that matters—* and doing it *constantly*. That is what good science is all about. Don't be led astray into a game of trivial pursuits.
2. Be a *professional* in the broadest interpretation of the word—and be one *constantly*, even when you're asleep and especially at cocktail parties.
3. Do *everything* in science with *enthusiasm*. We see too little of it in disciplines like ours that should inspire so much of it.
4. *Participate*—in professional societies, ethics committees, organizing committees, grant evaluation panels—all the great time-consuming infrastructure of science.
5. When other professionals (peers and colleagues) do something exceptional, *tell them* that you think so. We don't seem to do enough in science of what some psychologists call ''stroking''—and it costs so little.
6. *Enjoy*—enjoy being an active participant in the development of human understanding.

In the interest of a balanced presentation, however, I admit that periodically during the massive intellectual effort involved in creating this and the other volumes in the series, I have been tempted to explore a concept developed so exquisitely and so long ago by Lewis Carroll—that of stepping through a looking glass into a scientific wonderland where almost everything is reversed, where words can mean anything we say they mean, and where almost nothing is as it seems. On other occasions, I have been tempted to heed the insights of A. Square (1929) in his book *Flatland*, to see whether my perceptions of science and scientists are not similarly warped and do not also suffer from a two-dimensional narrowness of vision. I have resisted these temptations until now, but I can't withdraw from the stage without some feeble parting gesture toward irrational thinking.

As an introduction to a universe that can be labeled "fractured science," I am proposing "Sindermann's Laws of the Absolute Minimum," or "The Dangers and Pitfalls of Science in Little Square Boxes." In this misty wasteland (as I have explored it), small, almost illegible, signposts appear, scattered at random. On them are aphorisms, cute sayings, admonitions, Burma-Shave-like slogans, and other guidelines that are designed to lead scientists down dead-end paths or to poisoned water holes. Some can be rejected immediately as absurd, but others are almost plausible enough to form part of a *modus vivendi* for unsuspecting travelers. After some half-hearted culling, I am left with a list of eleven items (absolutely the last list of any kind that I will assemble for publication):

- Simplicity is natural; complexity is an invention of man and the Devil.
- Definition of a process implies that it must exist according to that definition.
- Definition of a process implies that it is controllable and predictable.
- Respect the absolute tyranny of uninformed opinion; when someone says, "This is the way the world is," and others do not object—believe it.

- Make up bad advice and follow it.
- Develop stupid rules and follow them blindly (examples could be "Move to another positon every five years" or "Never stay in an institution where you formerly occupied a position of power" or "Every move must be an upward one").
- Construct dumb theories and defend them irrationally.
- Cater to the bogus accumulated wisdom of advanced age.
- Do not underestimate the superficiality of understanding or the shallowness of interest of scientists on any topic.
- Believe in the obvious and reject the unlikely.
- Never hesitate to make that great conceptual leap from observed correlation of two events to pronouncement of a cause-and-effect relationship.

This list, if it serves no other purpose, should alert discerning scientists to the risks of trying to describe and codify the complex interpersonal strategies—the games—that appear during professional careers. The list should also disclose the narrowness of the trail to be followed by any self-proclaimed arbiter of rules that scientists live by.

But enough. The subject of interpersonal strategies in science has been a long-time hobby of mine, but it has now grown to monster proportions with an insatiable appetite and constantly expanding dimensions. It is time to kill it, and to let other, more rational voices be heard.

I will disappear with a final caveat about the subjectivity of most of the material presented in this book written primarily for new scientists. The volume is stuffed with neat guidelines designed to offer some assistance to upwardly mobile junior professionals. It should be obvious, though, that the upward path of every scientist will be different, and its personal components will also be different. One perceptive reviewer of early drafts of this book felt strongly that greater emphasis should have been placed on the *idealism* of science, which does not have to be abandoned in favor of career gains. To her, stressing the value of games tended to minimize the alternate routes to success that many good scientists have found and the pleasures they have derived from a very "human" occupation. I concur with this assessment and admit the deficiency; undoubtedly a more philosophical approach could have been taken, in the interest of a rounded exposition. This book on survival strategies certainly can't be filed on a library shelf labeled "Philosophy of Science," but it does express a viewpoint that is nonetheless a legitimate if somewhat pragmatic approach to the more personal side of the profession.

REFERENCES

Bartholomew, G.A., 1986, The role of natural history in contemporary biology, *Bioscience* 36(5):324–329.

Hadamard, J.S., 1945, *The Psychology of Invention in the Mathematical Field*, Princeton University Press, New Jersey.

Merton, R.K., 1968, The Matthew effect in science, *Science* 159:56–63.

Spinks, J.W.T., 1975, Gift of the gods: Some personal reminiscences and thoughts about creativity, *Chemistry in Canada* 27:21–24.

Square, A. [Edwin A. Abbott], 1929, *Flatland: A Romance of Many Dimensions*, Little, Brown & Co., Boston.

INDEX